W9-COT-162

What people are saying about *Let's Do Family Together* . . .

"Talk about changing your family legacy! That's exactly what Gary and Norma did—and you can, too! This book reveals all of their treasured secrets. Whether your family needs an overhaul or a tune-up, you won't want to miss out on this powerful message. It's authentic, practical, and grounded. You will simply love this book!"

—Drs. Les and Leslie Parrott, authors of *Saving Your Marriage Before It Starts*

"Gary Smalley has been my mentor and friend for the past fifteen years. I've heard him teach. I've watched him live. He practices what he preaches. This book is like the greatest hits of forty years of marriage ministry and over seventy years of life. I'm deeply grateful for this man."

—Ted Cunningham, pastor, Woodland Hills Family Church; author, *Fun Loving You* and *The Power of Home*

"Gary Smalley has spent a lifetime helping couples with marriage and family issues. In *Let's Do Family Together*, he looks back over his own family journey and shares the key elements that have guided him, Norma, and their children and grandchildren. This book provides a roadmap to having healthy family relationships and leaving a positive family legacy. It's a gold mine of practical relationship nuggets. I highly recommend it."

—Gary D. Chapman, PhD, author of *The Five Love Languages*

"The way you interact with your spouse and your children now can impact your family for generations to come. Gary Smalley understands this better than most, and he outlines seven key principles for making it happen in this excellent book. If you and your family want to embrace the journey together—both the highs and the lows—you need to read this!"

—Jim Daly, president, Focus on the Family, Colorado Springs, Colorado

"Gary Smalley, in *Let's Do Family Together*, has once again captivated the hearts of his readers with his vulnerable honesty and practical persuasion to give crystal clear insight into the building blocks of spiritually healthy families. Highlighting his own personal experiences, Smalley extracts real-life application and biblical understanding to the most critical issues that families deal with on a daily basis. In his pages, you will glean support and confidence to make choices that will honor God and those you love."

—Michelle Anthony, vice president and publisher of learning resources at David C. Cook; author of *Becoming a Spiritually Healthy Family, Spiritual Parenting, Dreaming of More for the Next Generation*, and *The Big God Story*

"Gary is a humble and honest man. He openly shares the stories of his family, both inspiring and embarrassing, to encourage all readers to experience the transformation of their families through God's grace. His story confirms that it is possible to build a healthy family despite our imperfections."

—Mark Batterson, lead pastor National Community Church, Washington D.C.; New York Times bestselling author of *The Circle Maker*

"Read the first chapter of this book, and you'll find an incredible story of a man who looked back at his family and life-story and had 'no regrets.' Read the *rest* of this outstanding book—written by my friend of friends, Gary Smalley, and his family—and you'll discover much more. Like specific, positive, life-changing ways to raise your own family and have 'no regrets' as well! Not perfection. Not formulas. But wisdom and hope, laughter and love, sound counsel and page after page of encouragement. This is a whole book of 'I can do that' head nods. That's because, without exaggeration, if there were a Mount Rushmore for the top marriage and family experts worldwide—Gary Smalley would be there. Learn from him, as our family has over the years. Read this book, and may God grant you and your family the blessings and closeness that Gary is able to look back on and that you can look forward to with your family."

—John Trent, PhD, Gary D. Chapman Chair of Marriage and Family Ministry and Therapy, Moody Theological Seminary, Chicago, Illinois

"Dr. Gary Smalley truly has a heart seeking Christ! Dr. Smalley and his wife, Norma, raised a family strongly founded on Christ-centered principles. His family story is a testament to the power of prayer and perseverance as well as the wisdom that comes along with it. Creating a family culture that makes a generational impact for the kingdom is invaluable, and Dr. Smalley has some great pointers on how to do that! He has done more to give me wisdom in my forty-three-year marriage than any other man on earth."

—Joe White, president of Kanakuk Ministries, Branson, Missouri

"Twenty-five years ago, Sheila and I attended a marriage seminar taught by Dr. Gary Smalley. As a young couple, we learned what it meant to show love and honor to one another. In this book, he pours a lifetime of experience and teaching into a work that will help us all learn how to pass on love and honor to future generations through seven simple steps. This book is a great practical tool for parenting."

—Jim McBride, executive pastor, Sherwood Baptist Church, Albany, Georgia; author of *Rite of Passage: A Father's Blessing*

"Gary Smalley has done it again! *Let's Do Family Together* is practical but profound. Learning and applying these seven keys will help your family grow healthy and strong!"

—Rod Loy, pastor, First Assembly of God, North Little Rock; author of *Three Questions, Immediate Obedience,* and *After the Honeymoon.*

LET'S DO
FAMILY
TOGETHER

— 7 —

KEYS FOR GENERATIONS
OF LOVE AND HONOR

GARY SMALLEY

Copyright © 2015 by Gary Smalley

ALL RIGHTS RESERVED

Published by Salubris Resources
1445 N. Boonville Ave
Springfield, Missouri 65802
www.salubrisresources.com

No part of this book may be reproduced, stored in a retrieval system, or transmitted in any form or by any means—electronic, mechanical, photocopy, recording, or otherwise—without prior written permission of the publisher, except for brief quotations used in connection with reviews in magazines or newspapers.

Cover design by Plain Joe Studios (www.plainjoestudios.com)
Interior formatting by Prodigy Pixel (www.prodigypixel.com)

Unless otherwise specified, Scripture quotations are taken from the Holy Bible, New International Version®, NIV®. Copyright © 1973, 1978, 1984, 2011 by Biblica, Inc. ™ Used by permission of Zondervan. All rights reserved worldwide.www.zondervan.com. The "NIV" and "New International Version" are trademarks registered in the United States Patent and Trademark Office by Biblica, Inc.™

Scripture quotations marked NLT are from the *Holy Bible*, New Living Translation. © 1996, 2004, 2007. Used by permission of Tyndale House Publishers, Inc., Wheaton, Illinois 60189. All rights reserved.

Scripture quotations marked The Message are from *The Message* by Eugene H. Peterson. © 1993, 1994, 1995, 1996, 2000. Used by permission of NavPress Publishing Group. All rights reserved.

Scripture quotations marked KJV are from the King James Version of the Bible, which is held in public domain.

ISBN: 978-1-68067-030-1

Printed in the United States of America

18 17 16 15 • 1 2 3 4

This book is dedicated to . . .

my kids and their spouses: Kari and Roger, Greg and Erin, and Michael and Amy;

my grandkids: Michael, Taylor, Hannah, Cole, Murphy, Reagan, Garrison, David, Annie, and Zoie Senait;

my future grandchildren's mates and great-grandchildren: may you be blessed to reflect the same love and honor in our family for generations to come;

and, of course, to my wife of fifty years, Norma Jean, who has done the best job of applying the seven keys of love and honor in our family.

CONTENTS

INTRODUCTION

A Love Letter—From Our Family to Yours

My wife, our three children, their mates, and our grandchildren all participated in each chapter of this book. You'll read about our failures and successes as we discovered and applied seven keys to raising a loving and happy family.

None of us are perfect. But what we enjoy as a family is wonderful. And we've been "Doing Family Together" for over forty-eight years! This book is built around proven keys we have used to raise our three kids. Now they're married and passing these same powerful truths on to their children.

How would you like to experience honor that leads to love with your extended family for many generations? Can you imagine generations of children and grandchildren who honor each other? In this book, you'll hear from three generations of our family. What we share has been tested by real life, including arrows, storms, and brushes with death—twice!

In fact, while writing this book, I even found myself on the receiving end of my family's care. We'll share more about that later.

If you feel urgency in these pages, it's because we have experienced what a loving family feels like, and we want the same for you!

Let's do family together!

—*Gary, Norma, and the Smalley/Gibson Families*

— 1 —

THE ATTACK

Wow! So this is what you feel just before you die.

Flat on my back in a damp meadow, with camouflage paint smeared on my face, I looked up to the sky. Little birds were flittering around in the silence. I whispered to myself, "This is it. Smalley, you're done. This is the last glimpse of earth you'll ever see."

I was hoping to live longer, but I said to God, "Thanks for a great life, my wife, and kids, and grandkids. I love them all. I wish I could say goodbye to them, but I can't."

The sense of calm was remarkable . . . and surprising.

It was difficult to talk, or even breathe. So I simply prayed, "Lord, I'll see you in a minute."

That's when an unfamiliar feeling settled on me from head to toe. I felt it go through me, slowly, to my core.

No Regrets

Yes, I ached to see my family, but I had no regrets. Of course there were things I wish I'd done differently as a husband, father, and grandfather. But forgiveness is real and so was this peace.

Had this moment come a few years earlier, my feelings might have been very different. I can't imagine moving out of this life without leaving behind a healthy family—not a perfect family, but generations who will continue to love each other.

Our family isn't perfect, but I couldn't be more thrilled with every one of them. Best of all, we enjoy each other.

As you and I begin this journey, here are two key questions we need to ask ourselves: What sort of person will I be? What kind of impact will I leave on my family?

If you can't answer those questions right now, don't worry. I couldn't either when I started out in marriage, parenting, or grandparenting!

The good news is, you can enjoy your family, no matter where you are in life and regardless of how you were raised. And your family can enjoy you!

Evidently, that autumn day in 2002 wasn't meant to be my last. My wife, Norma, certainly didn't think so.

Hunting

My friend Junior is a real outdoorsman and had been after me for years to go turkey hunting with him. I've always been fascinated by the idea but never tried it.

I'd just gotten home from a big conference and was exhausted. Junior knew I was back and called to ask me, once again, if I was ready to hunt.

"You know what?" I replied, "I can't think of any reason to say no. This could be a great way to recharge."

The next day began at 5:00 a. m. We drove for over an hour into the woods and out of cell-phone range.

"This is it," he said. "There's a turkey in here—lots of turkeys!"

We geared up in full camo and even rubbed on some green face paint. As we started marching through the thick woods, Junior offered to carry my gear since he could tell I was worn out. At well over six feet tall, he was like a giant puppy, eager to get to the secret clearing. I felt like an old hound dog.

The cool air and scent of autumn was refreshing. Hearing my expert guide imitate turkey calls and all sorts of other creatures was captivating. But hiking through fields, across creeks, and over fences was tougher than I expected.

So much for my day of rest!

The hill we started to climb was getting the best of me. It was a long, gradual slope, but had no path. Constantly high-stepping over branches and rocks was sapping my energy. Breathing became difficult, and the layers of camouflage fabric make me sweat. I had imagined turkey hunting as sitting in the woods, drinking coffee, and waiting.

"Gosh ... I'm really out of shape ..."

Stumbling to the top of the hill, the only sounds I could hear were my gasps for air.

Just then, a male turkey showed up about twenty-five yards away. I was breathing so loudly that Junior yelled at me in a whisper, "Shhh, quiet! You're gonna scare it off."

"I don't know what's happening . . . I can't breathe," I muttered.

But Junior was focused. "See where the turkey is?" he pointed. "When it goes behind this oak tree and comes out on the other side, shoot it."

As he handed me the gun, all my attention was fixed on that bird. As the turkey tiptoed out from behind the big tree, I squeezed the trigger.

Kickback

The blast was so powerful it knocked me onto my back. Or maybe I didn't have the strength to stand another second. My breathing tightened even more, and the pain in my chest paralyzed me.

This was more than exhaustion.

My guide ran back to me with excited news, "Hey, you shot a trophy turkey! It's an eleven-inch beard."

As he showed it to me I calmly said, "I'm sorry, I can't look right now. I'm having a heart attack." Blood was pushing against my lungs, and I could barely breathe.

"Not on my watch," Junior snapped with confidence, then ran back down the hill towards the truck.

During his absence, I realized I wouldn't be alive when he got back.

Life was pouring out of me, yet peace was overwhelming me. I totally relaxed and sighed, "Any second." And then I simply waited, taking it all in.

Junior had a different plan. I found out later that he's a fifth-degree black belt. He sprinted to the four-wheel-drive truck and somehow crashed his way back up the trail to the bottom of the hill. I heard him arrive and yell out to me as he ran up the hill.

Despite the fact that he was now carrying me towards

the truck, I knew I'd still be gone soon. And being carried like a bag of sand wasn't helping the situation.

Laid out in the back seat, still straining to catch one solid breath, our cell phones finally beeped back to life. Junior called 911. I dialed Norma just to say goodbye and tell her I loved her, one last time.

Holding On

"Hey," she answered. "Hold on, I've got somebody in the office here." Click.

I was on hold, and thought to myself, "Okay, I'll tell her I love her when she gets to heaven."

Long seconds passed. As she returned to the call I blurted, "Hon, I'm having a heart attack, and I don't know if I'll ever see you again, so I want you to know that I love you."

Seemingly unfazed, she asked, "Where are you?"

I tried to explain but could hardly talk. She jumped up, grabbed our son Greg who worked in our office and headed to the hospital.

About fifteen minutes later, a helicopter arrived for me. I was intrigued by all the commotion but still didn't expect to make it to the hospital alive. Despite the fact that my body began shaking, an unexpected sense of calm remained.

That was, until I was rolled into the emergency room.

Shaky

Norma and Greg rushed over and surprised me.

"Save your breath, save your energy. We know you love us,"

they said as the stretcher rolled me down the hall. Nearing the doors at the end of the hallway, Norma put her face into view and glared, "You listen to me. You are *not* dying. Do you hear me?"

I can remember laughing inside, hoping she could see the love in my eyes. *This is so her*, I thought. *Even now, she's telling me what to do.*

On the operating table I was still shaking like a strip of bacon on a hot pan. Every muscle in my body was trembling, including my heart. There I was, ready to receive life-saving care, and the doctor couldn't even get the I.V. in because of the muscle spasms!

"Please, Mr. Smalley, stop shaking," the doctor insisted. "I'm s-s-s-s-sorry. I'm not doing this on purpose." Then I said to God, "God, I can't stop this. You know what's happening to me. Would you stop the shaking?"

Stillness. The needle went in, and I went out.

Waking Up

While I was lying on my back during my first, and only, turkey hunt, I had surprising clarity about my life and my family.

I had no regrets, only love. I knew the Smalley family would honor and love each other after I was gone.

Can you imagine that feeling?

I want you to experience this same satisfaction in your family. And that's the remarkable treasure I get to share with you. I have so much good news to share, about your life and your forever.

Expecting More

I trace my heart attack, and other physical health issues, to stress from unmet expectations. Most of us go into marriage, parenting, and grandparenting with beautiful hopes and dreams. But what do we do when the quality of our marriage and family doesn't measure up?

Had I not discovered, by the grace of God, the seven keys you're about to read, my experience on that hunting trip would have been tragically different.

Instead of pain, I had peace. Instead of regret, I knew forgiveness. Instead of unmet expectations, I felt love. Instead of anger, I had harmony. Instead of treasuring my possessions, I treasured my family.

Instead of fear, I had faith.

Family and Life

There's lots of talk these days about the need for community. We do need community. But deep down we know the highest form of community is family. I didn't say the *easiest*, but it is the best and the most rewarding form.

Imagine a "community" of love and goodness that lasts for generations. This is what family is designed to be!

Over the past several months, my family has stepped up for me in ways I never dreamed. All eighteen of my family members have rallied around my Norma and me. Some of them even stayed all night in my hospital room to make sure I was alive in the morning.

I've never seen anything like their care and can't wait to share more about this experience.

The Big Question

What would life be like on this earth if the majority of people were free from anger and alive with love toward one another?

My childhood was pretty rough and certainly didn't offer me a model for marriage or parenting. I didn't have any clue about being a husband, or a dad, but did have a real hunger for a healthy family.

A couple miracles later, this hunger turned into a desire to help families all over the world. As it turns out, after parenting for over forty-eight years now, all eighteen of our family members use the seven keys on a daily basis.

Many people look at marriage gurus and think they have it all together. This book will prove that's not true. I'm not perfect, and I live in a family that's not perfect. Norma and I often wondered if, despite our best intentions, we were really screwing up our kids ... and even our grandkids!

IMAGINE A "COMMUNITY" OF LOVE AND GOODNESS THAT LASTS FOR GENERATIONS. THIS IS WHAT FAMILY IS DESIGNED TO BE!

I can assure you that if there was hope for our family, there's hope for your marriage and your family.

Let's Do Family Together

I want to explain, and let my family share, the keys that worked for us, and I want to help you apply these keys to your family and your life.

If we don't fight together against the attacks on the family unit, we're going to keep experiencing the same cycle of painful results. Instead of dysfunction passing through generations—why not health, honor, and love?

Norma and my kids helped make me a better husband, father, and grandfather. So I want you to meet them in this book and hear their stories. In fact, I'll say this right up front: Norma gets most of the credit for parenting our three children.

People often shy away from steps to improve their marriage and family because it can feel like we're walking through a minefield. The principles we'll share here will help you take steps to change the dynamics of your family, no matter how your relationships seem.

Is your spouse the polar opposite of you?

Are your kids angry? Grandkids distant?

Are you withdrawn from your parents or grandparents?

As a single parent, do you wonder if you'll ever remarry and have a solid marriage?

Are you part of a blended family and wondering how to create harmony?

Aunts, uncles, nieces, nephews, and cousins—do you want to see your extended family heal and grow?

As a grandparent, do you wonder about being cared for in your later years? I can't wait to share what I've experienced while writing this book!

I'm giving you the tools that can change your life and impact five generations of your family and beyond!

Of course, no one is expected to live these principles perfectly. The idea is to grow a lifestyle that creates harmony, love, and honor.

This is what works in a wonderful, imperfect family.

Hold on tight to this book as you read. This is me, and Norma, and my family circled around you, cheering you on.

—— 2 ——

THE ROCK OF HONOR

When I was a kid, diamonds were the furthest things from my mind. But somehow I remember that back then only diamonds of colorless clarity were considered valuable. Yellow diamonds were considered less desirable and sold for much lower prices. Then at some point, for reasons beyond my understanding, these yellowish stones became prized more highly than their clear cousins.

How in the world did that change in value happen? Pretty simple. Someone took a fresh look at these unique gems and saw rare beauty. As more and more people changed their minds, these bits of earth were elevated to a place of high worth.

The same principle of value applies to every person in your family. One of the most important decisions I ever made was to look for, and honor, the many wonderful qualities of my wife and our kids. But like the yellow diamond, it took me a while to find this truth and to raise my family's value to its God-given value. They are all yellow diamonds now!

---
(1)

I will learn to highly honor and love each family member.

Honoring Life

Life is all about relationships and everything else is just details. As a marriage and family pastor, I first discovered the concept of honor by observing over 500 Baylor University students. I had the opportunity to teach them on Sundays, and I met with many during the week at the student center.

These young couples could fall deeply in love with great emotional affection for one another, but within a year I'd watch them fall out of love and break up the relationship. I also watched couples in our church who stopped loving each other. Many chose to walk away from what could have been a wonderful lifetime of marriage, parenting, and grandparenting.

I felt like a scientist, listening and observing. Couples were affectionate towards one another as long as they valued their partner and knew *why* they highly valued them. But if they stopped valuing, they lost their affection.

So I began to practice with them, sharing how they could write an "honor list." It wasn't long before we discovered major improvement in the affection of those couples.

Then I took the concept home and began to watch my affection for my wife grow in amazing ways. The same happened in my wife and three kids! Highly honoring each other became the cornerstone of my teaching, counseling, and writing.

I watched some of those Baylor students fall in love and learn to intentionally value each other. Four decades of marriage later, they're still affectionate and enjoy a strong relationship.

One way of approaching this idea of honor is to simply agree with God, and value what He values. The main reason I'm committed to Norma and our family is because God values them, just as He values every family, in all shapes and sizes.

This is the main reason I wanted to write this book. I highly value, "Yellow Diamond," my family members. Therefore, I highly love my future generations because I want them to enjoy the same type of love we now have.

Jesus made it pretty clear about our worth when He pointed to the little birds flying around: "Are you not much more valuable than they?" Jesus asked His disciples (Matthew 6:26). And of course, because God loves us more than we can comprehend, He sent Jesus to reveal this to us with His words, actions, and life.

When you see your spouse, family, and yourself as valuable from God's perspective, it's much easier to begin honoring each person.

What Is Honor?

Honor, according to the Merriam-Webster dictionary, is "respect that is given to someone who is admired—one whose worth brings respect or fame." In the Smalley house, our definition is "placing high value on people, places, and things."

Imagine I handed you a glimmering yellow diamond the size of your hand and asked you to take care of it for me. How would you treat that stone? Where would you keep it? How would you handle it when checking on its condition? How often would you think about it?

How much more valuable are the hearts of your family?

When you make the decision to value people like God does, your eyes and heart will begin to open to the beautiful treasures around you. Yes, even those people who've hurt you, or who might be driving you nutty right now.

> BEING ABLE TO LOVE OTHERS GROWS FROM THE VALUE THAT WE PLACE UPON THEM. (NOT THE OTHER WAY AROUND!)

In other words, real love follows honor. Being able to love others grows from the value that we place upon them. (Not the other way around!)

If you honor someone with your thoughts, looking for and thinking about their value, you tend to reflect God's character. You'll be more loving, patient, joyful, and compassionate.

The way you feel towards a person is determined by how much value you place upon them.

Honor moves us to forgive, to have more open communication, and to truly care for the needs of others. Placing high value on every member of your family brings more peace, joy, and love into your own life.

Jesus said something crucial about our hearts, and about this first key of honor, "Where your treasure is, there your heart will be also" (Matthew 6:21). As we treasure our family members as highly valuable, heartfelt affection and love will grow toward each member!

Honor in Real Life

You might be thinking, "How am I supposed to honor someone when I'm so angry and disappointed with them?"

Honor recognizes that everyone has faults, blind spots,

and "logs in their eyes" (Matthew 7:4 NLT). Nobody's perfect. This includes you and me! Like diamonds, we each have our own flaws and yet, we are still valuable.

The real secret is to discover the unique value within each person. I'll show you how to start making a list about each family member. As your list grows, you'll start to feel the amazing value of each family member.

God showed us His love and the high value He places on us when He sent His Son to lay down His life for you and me. Think about that. He honored us first, before we could ever honor Him. He loved us first, before we could love Him. I'm so grateful that God didn't wait for us to be worthy of His love.

So let's be clear, honor is a choice you make to improve your relationships, before your relationships improve! I didn't say this was easy, but it will change you and your family for generations.

Honoring Yourself

Lack of honor is one of the root causes for the evil we see in society. People who don't honor themselves as God's beloved are more likely to treat themselves poorly and to hurt others.

Norma and I often said to our kids when they were growing up, "Honor God and His creation." Then we would remind them that we are part of God's creation. We all need reminders of this truth, because God's love for us is the foundation of honor.

Jesus told us to love others as we love ourselves. Think about that! Understanding our own value to God is essential.

I've accepted my weaknesses and flaws. God loves me. And He loves you. Let's accept the value God has chosen to place on us. Only then will we begin to see the value of other people and join in with God to lift others up!

Honoring Your Mate

Just like someone made the decision to place high value on yellow diamonds, you can decide to honor your spouse. As you do, you'll find more and more to treasure.

Let's begin with a very practical step you can take. But I need to warn you, this is so basic many people don't take the time to actually do this exercise.

Simply get paper and pen, or your gizmo of choice, and start making a list of the positive qualities you value about your mate. I say to *start* a list, because this may be difficult at first, especially if you feel hurt or angry towards that person

Start your list of values anyway.

My Mate

Here's part of a list I've been building for over five decades, about my wife, Norma. (I have dozens of pages!) These *valuables* will help point your heart in the right direction to create your own list.

- Passion—she's passionately committed to strengthening marriages and families
- Steadfast—she's unwavering and firm in purpose
- Integrity—she's honest and tightly adheres to moral principles
- Loyal—she'll go to the "ends of the earth" for her friends
- Intuitive—she values and pays attention to her "gut" feeling

- Faithful—she has a very devoted relationship with the Lord
- Strong—she has a quiet strength to influence people
- Fair—she's committed to being fair and not playing favorites
- Playful—she's young at heart
- Humble—she doesn't need the spotlight
- Dream-maker—she's committed to making other people's dreams come true

When you take time to consider, and write, how valuable your spouse really is, it's amazing how your heart and mind begin to shift. And that's the point of this exercise.

Building your list helps you realize you're married to someone extremely valuable, even when you feel frustrated or angry. Okay—especially when you're frustrated or angry!

For some reason, it's easier for people to carry around a "hurt list" or "pain in the neck" list with items like, sloppy, selfish, annoying laugh, or snores like a rhino.

Honor means choosing to focus on the positive qualities we value.

The Why

I hate doing marriage seminars when my wife's not speaking to me. When Norma and I get out of sync, or when I've said something hurtful, why would I pursue her and try to repair the damage? Honor.

She's way too valuable not to pursue—and I can name

many specific reasons! Our marriage is way too valuable to me. Our marriage is valuable for our kids. Norma's a wonderful mom.

HONOR MEANS CHOOSING TO FOCUS ON THE POSITIVE QUALITIES WE VALUE.

Our kids are valuable. Our marriage is valuable to our grandkids—and our great grandkids, and generations to come!

Over the years, when Norma and I have gotten sideways about an issue, I start reading my honor list, and my attitude towards her immediately begins to change. Sometimes I even get teary-eyed, reminding myself of the awesome person I've married.

When I decide to switch from my negative, dishonoring thoughts to honoring thoughts, the change in my emotions is miraculous.

I hope you'll take a moment to begin your list right now. Why am I so insistent? Because honor will bring healing to a troubled marriage and growth to a good marriage.

Honor for a Woman

Early in my ministry, I started interviewing men and women about relationships. That's when I became convinced all wives have a built-in marriage manual!

The real eye-openers came from my conversations with women—an estimated 60,000 in groups and individual discussions from all over the world. Most often, I asked this question to married women, "On a scale of zero to ten, how satisfying is your marriage?"

They would answer, *four, eight,* or *zero*—I've even heard some "minus" scores!

Then I followed up with a second question, "What would need to happen in your marriage for it to improve, so the number would go up closer to ten?"

Every woman on earth knows the answer to that question. Without exception, they said, "If we just had better communication."

Being a typical man, I would respond, "But what do you mean by better communication?"

And that's where I started learning about honoring my wife with words and actions—and the importance of communication. What I learned about relationships in school was important, but much of it was theory. I learned far more from interviewing and taking massive amounts of notes.

Sometimes, the most profound answer I heard was silence.

"What does your husband do to improve your marriage on a regular basis?" This question almost always generated a blank look. Sure, most women could name a few examples, but these seemed to fall short of what could be happening in their marriage.

Norma was expressing those same needs and wants at home. This is painful to admit, but I figured she was just selfish and needy. And all of a sudden it clicked. I'm married to one of these women!

Man Talk

Here's where I need to have a little chat with the husbands. Men, you and I are more alike than we realize. In many ways, you're a lot slower to catch on about relationships than your wife.

You might think your wife is being whiny, nagging, or even moody. I bet you a hundred bucks you're missing some relational keys that are painfully obvious to your wife. And that's humbling to admit.

God created differences in men and women so husbands and wives could help each other. Honoring each other means honoring our differences, too. As you commit, or re-commit, to honor your wife, realize that she has valuable perspective and insights that you don't have.

For example, I'd tell Norma I wanted to invest in something, and she'd often say, "Nah, don't do that. I don't feel right about it."

Initially, I would react defensively and tell her, "You don't even know anything about this financial opportunity."

Almost every time we had that discussion, I discovered she was right!

Unfortunately, I've made many major decisions against her counsel. In each case, I was absolutely sure my view was correct, and her view was ... not worthy of honor.

Wonderful balance and wisdom has come into my life because of my wife—much more than I can relate in this book or several books.

As I write this, I realize that at any time during the day, we can completely change our view of our wives by deciding they are "yellow diamonds." You can choose to focus on the many valuable qualities of your wife.

Honor your wife by honoring her feelings and perspectives.

Honoring Your Kids

I thoroughly enjoyed making a fool out of myself with my kids, and I still do with my grandkids.

When our kids were growing up, I used to go into the living room, or wherever they were, get down on my knees and cry out "I'm not worthy! I'm not worthy!"

They'd roll their eyes and say, "Dad, what are you doing?"

I'd continue, "I can't believe I get to live in the same home with the most valuable kids on earth. Wow! I'm so privileged to have you as my children."

"Dad, you're so weird," they would say.

Did this over-the-top behavior affect them? Absolutely! I hear them repeat the same words today—and hear the same responses from my grandkids!

I've quizzed them all a thousand times, "What's the greatest thing in life?" And they would answer, "Dad, we know ... honor God. Honor His creation, people, and things. You don't have to keep telling us."

> HONOR YOUR WIFE BY HONORING HER FEELINGS AND PERSPECTIVES.

How do my kids and grandkids live today? They honor God, God's creation, people, and things. Especially wonderful is how they honor Norma and me—and teach us about honor!

A STORY FROM OUR GRANDSON MICHAEL

After high school, my parents went to the mission field, and I chose to stay stateside and live with my grandparents. So, when I was living with them, Grandpa had this weird desire to have our entire family eat healthy. I'm not really the best eater. I like fried foods and funnel cakes.

Sometimes he would come up to me, pinch my side, and I could sense that he was thinking *you really want to have another dessert?* To me it was totally dishonoring.

During that time, it was really hard for me because my parents were on the mission field. Sometimes Grandpa said, "You do realize that you're possibly going to have a heart attack when you're twenty-one?" He said this over and over and over.

So finally, I just came up to him and said, "You know what, Grandpa? I really feel like you tell everybody that you honor your grandkids and that we're best friends, but what kind of best friend pinches your side and says, 'Are you really going to have that second helping?'"

He looked at me and answered, "You know what? You're absolutely right. It's not my job to be your food policeman. It's my job to honor you and be your grandpa."

That meant so much to me. And I liked it even more when he asked me to forgive him.

Value in Detail

Tell your kids they're valuable. And tell them precisely why they're valuable to you—as many reasons as you can think up and write down!

When I visit my granddaughter Annie, she greets me with a loud "Grandpa!" and jumps into my arms. After a few moments I'll ask her, "Why do I love you so much?"

And she'll answer with a big smile, "Because I'm Chinese?"

"That's one reason," I say. "Gosh, why else?"

"Because I'm a girl and I'm seven-years-old?"

"Yes, that's another reason."

And she'll go through a list of several more things, and I'll add a couple new ways I value her. What a thrill, and honor, to see her heart drink it all in.

You might not be a big goofball like me, but you get the point. Think about the valuable qualities of every member of your family, write them down, and make a big deal about them—often!

Honor is even more crucial in blended families because they're a smash-up of valuable people with valuable feelings and perspectives. Sure, every family is a variety-pack, but blended families crash together at high speed.

> **"**
>
> HONOR IS EVEN MORE CRUCIAL IN BLENDED FAMILIES BECAUSE THEY'RE A SMASH-UP OF VALUABLE PEOPLE WITH VALUABLE FEELINGS AND PERSPECTIVES.

Your kids are listening, even when they're rolling their eyes.

Honor Their Future

We learned, through trial and error, to intentionally nurture the particular strengths and talents in all our kids.

Norma and I would tell our daughter, Kari, "You'd be a great school teacher." And guess what? That's exactly what she became.

We'd tell Michael, "You'd be a great writer and counselor." In college, he majored in journalism and in drama. And he's my favorite speaker—hilariously funny and delivers great content.

We told Greg all the time, "You'd be a great lawyer and counselor." He chose counseling and is helping thousands of couples.

> **MISTAKES AND BLUNDERS ARE AN OPPORTUNITY TO DEVELOP EVEN MORE HONOR.**

When your kids and grandkids, nieces and nephews, catch the concept of honor, don't be surprised if they hold you accountable when someone is being been disrespected. They're starting to participate in the beauty, and safety, of a family unit.

"Dad, I heard what you just said to Mom. How do you feel about that?"

My twelve-year-old son, Greg, had the courage to ask me that question. You see, awareness of honor raises the bar in your family. You want to nurture a family who values each other enough to speak up.

I swallowed my pride and replied, "I hate that I dishonored your mom, my wife, with my words."

On more than one occasion, he'd ask me, "Dad, is this how you want me to treat my wife when I get married?"

He knew what dishonor was because we taught and demonstrated honor on a consistent basis. Another wonderful thing about highly valuing your family members is that perfection isn't required. In fact, mistakes and blunders are an opportunity to develop even more honor.

A STORY WITH "BITE" FROM OUR GRANDSON DAVID

Once, when I was twelve, a few of my friends in the neighborhood were all on a trampoline jumping together. At some point our jumping turned into wrestling, and I love to wrestle.

We were all matching up with each other in the middle of the trampoline and trying to pin each other down like a real wrestling match.

The good news is that I've had a lot of practice at wrestling because of the summers I've spent at Kanakuk Kamp in Branson, Missouri. The bad news is that I pinned my friend really quickly, which upset this friend (a girl) and she bit me! It happened so fast! I felt really strong, but then I felt a sharp pain on my arm. This girl was biting me!

I was so mad that I really wanted to bite her back. But then I remembered something my dad says all the time. (Apparently my grandpa used to say it to my dad all the time, too!)

It starts with a question, "What's the most important thing in life?" All the Smalley kids know the answer to this question! Honor God, honor others, and honor yourself.

Even though I wanted to bite her back, I knew it would be dishonoring. So I chose to head straight home and show my dad what had happened.

My dad hugged me and made sure I was okay. I told him that I wanted to bite her but didn't because I honor people. Then he hugged me even harder!

***

Honoring Grandkids and Their Parents

Kids can say some really mean words. So can grown-ups.

Several years ago, I was in my son Greg's house, and his son

Garrison was picking on his adopted sister, Annie. This kind of behavior really gets under my skin because it's a destructive form of dishonor.

As the teasing became more intense, I kept waiting for Greg to say something. And all of a sudden, I exploded with "Well, you know, he's really in charge of Annie, like a parent."

My grandson immediately ran to his room, crying all the way. I got one of those looks from Greg and "nice going, Dad." I felt terrible.

So I immediately jumped up and apologized to Garrison, telling him that he was way too valuable to be spoken to like that. He still had his head buried into a pillow, sobbing.

HONOR GOD, HONOR OTHERS, AND HONOR YOURSELF.

He wouldn't respond to me, but that was okay. My apology was based on honor. And whether they show it at the time or not, your kids are learning about honor. Not so much the words you speak, but the actions you take to demonstrate value toward each other. And when you mess up, you apologize, because families are worthy of honor.

The next morning I asked him, "Did you ever forgive me?"

"Oh, Grandpa, yeah, I forgave you last night. It's okay."

It's not pleasant to go to someone, especially a child or grandchild, and admit you were wrong and ask, "Will you forgive me?"

Your actions speak louder than your words, even the mean words that slip out from time to time.

Generations of Honor

Now that Norma and I are grandparents, we have the privilege of seeing honor flow through three generations.

When our kids were in their twenties, they began to share how much they appreciated my embarrassing "I'm not worthy" speeches, and other often-repeated Smalley family discussions.

For example, I used to ask them, "Is there anything you can do to lose my love? Anything?"

They would wonder, "What if I go to prison?"

I would say, "No, if you go to prison, I'll be there visiting you, bringing you cakes, but I'll never stop loving you. I'm your dad. I am who I am, and I'll always love you, no matter what you do. You can reject me. You can pull away from anything I believe. It doesn't matter what you do, I'll always love you, and I'll be there if you need me."

A few years ago I heard our son Michael asking his son Cole, "Is there anything you can do to stop me from loving you?"

Hearing these question and answer sessions repeated in another generation brings such joy to my heart. Even better, Norma and I know this will continue in our family long after we're gone.

GREG CAN'T TELL THIS STORY WITHOUT TEARS

When I was doing my internship in psychology, we heard the sad news that a father in our neighborhood had left his family. One of his kids was a six-year-old girl who was a friend of my daughter, Taylor.

One weekend, these two girls were at our house playing upstairs, when the play turned to a loud argument.

"No, they won't." "Yes, they will," back and forth.

Taylor, with her friend, ran downstairs and announced, "Daddy, I've got a question for you. She says that you and Mommy are going to divorce because her parents are divorcing. But I told her that would never happen. Who is right?"

My heart broke. Turning to her friend, I gently said "I have to admit that Taylor's right. Her Mommy and I are never going to divorce. Marriage is extremely important to us. We're committed to each other for our whole lives."

Taylor stuck her tongue out at the little girl and ran back upstairs. But her little friend asked to sit with me and watch the football game for a while. After a few minutes of watching TV, I broke the silence, "I wonder if Taylor is missing you upstairs?"

As she scooted off the couch, she looked at me and asked, "Do you think it would be possible . . . for me to come back sometimes, and pretend that you're my Daddy . . . and just sit with you?"

That statement made such a big impact on my life. It really energized my heart to stop the painful cycle of divorce.

Where Is Your Heart?

Remember the words of Jesus, "Where your treasure is, there your heart will be also" (Matthew 6:21; Luke 12:34). Affection for your spouse and kids, and your extended family, will continue to grow as you maintain an awareness of each person as a priceless treasure.

Again, this is a choice, and it might seem impossible if you feel anger and resentment toward them. That's why I'm encouraging you to not only start your written list of valuable qualities, but to keep it in front of you, and add to it as often as you can.

Criticisms and hurtful words will begin to be replaced with affirmations of that person's value. Think about them as "yellow diamonds" and discover how your affection grows.

When you invest time, energy, words, and actions to treasure someone in this way, your heart will grow in love for them.

AFFECTION FOR YOUR SPOUSE AND KIDS, AND YOUR EXTENDED FAMILY, WILL CONTINUE TO GROW AS YOU MAINTAIN AN AWARENESS OF EACH PERSON AS A PRICELESS TREASURE.

Honoring Your Future

"Is there anything you could do to make me stop loving you?"

What if you had this same honoring conversation with your spouse?

This is where generations of honor begin. In my decades of counseling couples, the stories I've heard would make your hair fall out. (Mine did.)

Yet all these families went from having no honor and no love, to enjoying high honor and love.

It all started with a decision.

Honor is choosing to notice and care for the amazing

treasures God has placed inside your family.

If all this high-value talk still feels a bit mysterious, or impossible, that's okay. I have many more practical keys to share.

— 3 —

OPENING CLOSED HEARTS

"You can tell me if I'm messing this up."

Imagine your sixth-grade school teacher had announced this on the first day of class. How would you feel about the learning environment? Would you feel free to ask questions or be more willing to admit you were struggling with a concept?

As a parent, I repeated this invitation countless times to our three kids. *"You can tell me if I'm messing this up as a parent anytime you want." "I'm open to hearing what you think about how I'm parenting you." "I look to you as experts in knowing what you need in order to feel love. So, feel free to give me suggestions on how you would like to be raised. I want us to do family together."*

At first, this admission might seem like a sign of weakness. After all, we're supposed to have it all together as parents—and children can smell fear, right?

No one has it all figured out. Honesty is the first step in creating a family environment that feels safe.

Once, when my son Greg was a teenager, I asked him to stop listening to one of Billy Joel's songs. Greg asked me why. He knew he wouldn't be punished or criticized, as long as he was respectful. He then asked me if I would be willing to listen to the song. I knew the right thing to do was gather the facts and honor his request.

THE SAFER A PERSON FEELS WITH YOU, THE MORE THEY'RE ATTRACTED TO BUILDING A DEEPER RELATIONSHIP WITH YOU.

So I listened to *An Innocent Man.* I actually liked the lyrics, because they're about a girl who is criticizing her current boyfriend for what her former boyfriend did to her. I told Greg why I liked the song, and we had a rich discussion about it. I was so grateful my kids felt safe enough to ask Norma and me about anything.

Safety Opens Closed Hearts

Safety is a part of honor. The reason we want our family members to feel safe is because we honor them. We value their perspectives, thoughts, emotions, questions, and convictions—even when they differ from ours.

My two sons, Greg and Michael, have discovered one of my favorite concepts: The safer your family members feel with you, the stronger your loving relationship grows. A safe relationship is a relationship where everyone feels safe to share their thoughts and feelings without fear.

But one way we create an un-safe zone and closed hearts is by trying to change our mate or our children, mainly by criticizing who they have become or who we think they are becoming.

Here are some themes you may never have considered that are powerful and life-changing.

1. Unsafe Change

The only person you can change is yourself. Safety is built when you stop trying to change your spouse or kids to make yourself happier and start taking responsibility for your own quality of life.

The greatest lesson I ever learned from my family was that my own thoughts will lead to my personal quality of life. People, places, and things will not make a person truly happy.

Have you ever felt the pressure of someone expecting you to change? Whether well-meaning or not, the sensation is deflating and can lead to resentment. When someone is not an example of the kind of change they want to see in you, are you likely to communicate more openly and honestly? Will you share your struggles and emotions?

Of course not! When your marriage becomes an unsafe place, you naturally don't want to be there anymore.

If you stop trying to change your mate, they will immediately feel a little bit safer. The safer they feel, the safer your children feel, and the safer your grandkids feel.

Consider this: The safer a person feels with you, the more they're attracted to building a deeper relationship with you. Best-friend relationships and rock-solid commitments naturally develop where safety exists.

You are secure to share your heart with a person when you feel safe and unafraid of being ridiculed. Again, this goes back to a foundation of honor and unconditional love.

2. "Conditional" Is Not Safe

For the first thirty-eight years of our marriage, I tried to change two areas of Norma's behavior. I believed if she would just change those two areas, I'd be happier and our marriage would be stronger.

One of the areas was the way we ate. Our diet seemed unhealthy to me. The second was that we didn't exercise together. Or more bluntly, I exercised; she didn't.

Part of the reason Norma wasn't more active was because her knee was injured in a car accident when she was in high school. She, and many doctors, tried to explain the chronic pain to me, but I couldn't relate. Or maybe I just didn't want to.

I tried so many different ways to argue and debate how healthy exercise would be for her. I offered frequent "encouragements" for us to eat healthier foods and often quoted the latest medical research.

Every time I brought up the diet subject, I actually expected Norma to say, "Wow! Thank you for sharing that information with me!"

After all, I wanted our senior years to be active and enjoyable—what was wrong with that?

Instead of helping her and our marriage, I was really creating an unsafe environment. She felt unaccepted by me. She felt judged and unloved. Norma was carrying around all those feelings, and I had no clue. Conditional love is not safe.

When the topic of food or exercise came up, we would usually get into an escalated argument. You would think I would have caught on earlier, but I seized the opportunity every time, thinking, *Well, the previous 300 attempts didn't work, but this next one probably will.*

AMAZING GRACE AND SAFETY

One afternoon, in the middle of one of my oh-so-helpful lectures, our son Greg walked into our home. He was thirty-five years of age, a psychologist, and excited about what he was discovering about relationships.

"Hey, Dad," he said, "I'm working on some new research and I want to share something with you. Why don't you come out in the front yard with me?"

"I'm really busy here. We've got an important conversation happening," I replied.

"It's only going to take a minute," Greg said calmly. And into the yard we went.

"Dad, you said you'd like me to teach you the stuff I'm learning on improving marriages, and the reason we're able to help couples reverse their plans to divorce in four days. One of the concepts is: Get off your mate's case and take responsibility for the quality of your own life."

Greg and I had discussed his research and seminars before, but it hadn't penetrated my skull—or my heart. My mindset was clear and logical: if Norma doesn't change, I'm not going to be happy. Therefore, I need to help her change.

So Greg spent some time explaining it again. "I'm telling you, this is the truth, and it works. Why don't you just try it?" This was a tough conversation for both of us, but we felt safe to talk about anything.

I took a deep breath. "Okay, so what do I need to do here?"

"Make a commitment within yourself to stop trying to change Mom. You believe you can't be happy until she changes, but that's not true. The key is for you to change your own attitude, simply change your own thoughts."

GENERATIONAL SAFETY

Well, I asked for it. Remember my invitation? *"You can tell me if I'm messing this up."*

Sure, I was talking about parenting and never imagined I would receive marriage advice from my kids. But this is what safety is all about. Greg, Kari, and Michael feel safe to express themselves to Norma and me, and we feel the same way.

Safety spreads through families and generations.

HONORING SAFETY

Shortly after this heart-to-heart with my son, an idea popped into my head about how I could change my behavior and begin to restore a sense of honor with Norma.

I invited her to a special dinner at a nice restaurant. Halfway through the meal I said, "I know you're wondering why I'm doing this tonight or what special occasion this might be."

I continued, "The reason I've invited you to dinner is because I've been sinning against you for thirty-eight years."

Her eyes got as big as our dinner plates. "What have you been doing for thirty-eight years?"

With a humble voice, I answered, "I've been correcting you, pressuring you, and trying to get you to change in two areas, and I've really, really . . . I've been wrong. I'm here tonight to ask you to forgive me, if you can."

She accepted my apology but was skeptical. After thirty-eight years she probably expected this shift in attitude would last about three days. Thankfully, she was wrong.

Jesus said we must get the log out of our own eye before trying to take a speck out of someone else's eye (Matthew 7:4 NLT). This experience caused me to see that verse in a fresh way.

Of course, I still had the urge to offer my usual commentary and suggestions, but my desire to honor my wife and make her feel safe was stronger. Besides, there were plenty of "logs" in my own eyes—flaws in my own character and behavior. I actually stopped blaming everyone and everything for making me unhappy.

WALKING SAFELY

About four years from the "Dad, you're messing this up" conversation, Norma called me at the office.

"Want to join me for lunch?"

"Sure," I said, "where are you going to eat?"

"Let's go to that new place we saw the other day. And bring your tennis shoes."

"What do we need those for?" I asked.

As we met in the parking lot, I finally got the answer to my question. "Well, I've been exercising—walking every day but not telling you. I didn't want to say anything because I was afraid you'd start in again."

I nodded, "Yeah, I can see why you would think I would criticize you."

This was another opportunity for me to realize how deeply I had hurt Norma in all those years of trying to make her change. She didn't even feel safe enough to tell me about her walks and the healthy changes she was making!

What are you keeping from your spouse, simply because you don't feel safe? Now consider what your mate is not sharing with you. That's why fostering safety is so important in a family relationship. And it starts by stopping: We must stop trying to change the people we love.

After our healthy lunch we set out on our walk. I was amazed at Norma's brisk pace! At one point she stopped and grabbed her knee. "Ugh, my knee is screaming at me today."

"Wow!" I said, "We don't have to walk now. Let's rest on this bench."

"No, I told this knee yesterday, 'I don't care how much you hurt. If I have to, I will drag you down the road.'"

My jaw dropped. Who was this motivated power walker? She was someone who felt safe enough to try new things—safe enough to stretch a bit for her family . . . and for herself.

SAFE THINKING

Change, in both of us, began when I stopped trying to change Norma. My thinking shifted from "I can only be happy if she changes" to "I choose to honor the many valuable qualities in my wife, and help her feel safe with me."

Safety is building a place where you're not afraid of being criticized.

Years ago there was a popular country song, with a title I'll paraphrase: *How can I kiss the lips that chew my butt all day?*[1]

Admit it. That's a pretty powerful word-picture of how a marriage can be destroyed when a spouse feels unsafe . . . and unloved.

SAFETY IS BUILDING A PLACE WHERE YOU'RE NOT AFRAID OF BEING CRITICIZED.

Have you ever wondered why certain topics escalate so quickly into arguments? When people don't feel safe, accepted, and honored, they experience fear. They withdraw. And they become angry.

In the following chapters, we'll talk more about the subject of anger and forgiveness. But hopefully you now recognize how someone in your marriage needs to change.

And it's not your spouse.

3. Single and Safe

If you're a single parent, creating a safe environment for your family is so important. As you understand and practice honor, you'll be more aware of unhealthy relationships and be able to steer clear of trouble.

My son Michael and his wife, Amy, have helped many single, divorced, and separated parents. Here's some perspective from Amy:

> If you're not really careful, broken relationships will bring out the very worst in you. So arm yourself with this reminder: "What would doing the right thing look like here?"
>
> You'll have many opportunities to be negative and react with anger. But you still have to do the right thing, and the right thing is not to blame, shame, or criticize. Honor your kids, and honor yourself, by avoiding negativity.

As you become aware of the danger of unsafe relationships, you'll be better equipped to spot a heathy person as a potential mate. Please remember, if a person doesn't honor you before marriage, they're extremely unlikely to honor you after marriage.

4. A Safe House

Do your kids, or grandkids, feel safe to share their feelings, hopes, and fears? Not just physically protected but emotionally free in their relationship with you?

Children can sense when their parents feel safe with each

other—and when they don't. The wonderful gift of acceptance begins with marriage and spills over to the whole family.

Here are some observations a few of my grandchildren recently shared:

> **Michael:** I appreciate Grandma and Grandpa just getting on their grandkids' level. When texting first started, they were really into it and wanted to communicate with us that way. They both got on Facebook so we could stay in touch in that way, too!

> **Murphy:** Our grandparents never looked down on us. They were never like, "Oh, I'm so much wiser than you . . . I have all this wisdom. Hear it and follow it exactly." They found subtle ways to give their wisdom to us, and in a way that was relatable, like taking us out to lunch and sharing their heart. It was really important to know that they actually cared about us and wanted to spend time with us.

> **Taylor:** When my boyfriend unexpectedly broke up with me, I remember both of my grandparents calling the very next day and encouraging me. They told me a lot of their love story that I had never heard before—using it to kind of point me to the Lord and telling me to trust that He has a plan.

> **Hannah:** I remember every single time I would see my grandpa when I was younger, he would say, "So what new dreams are in your heart? I'd like for you to share with me all these things. I want to pray for

them and help you watch them grow." I told Grandpa about a year ago that I wanted to go to Alaska by bus, and his reaction was, "Oh, go Hannah! Have fun!" Instead of saying, "What the heck are you thinking?" he said, "Oh, can I go with you? We'll go together!"

Taylor: I really love Grandma's personality. She's kind of like this little—firecracker. You wouldn't look at her and think that she's this strong firecracker, but she really can be. But she can also be a quiet encourager.

Hannah: To this day, Grandma still texts me once a week, asking me how she can pray for me. And so, it's been really cool, just over the last couple years, being able to come back to her when I see her in person and say, "Hey, this prayer was totally answered," and I thank her so much for doing that.

Michael: I think people don't really realize exactly how wise Grandma is. Grandpa's obviously in the spotlight a lot, but I think a lot of the stuff that Grandpa has come up with is really because of Grandma. She has a quiet strength, and I love that about her. And she's funny; she's really funny.

Taylor: With my dad, one idea that he's always drilled into our heads is "guard your heart above anything else." And that's definitely the way Grandpa thinks. He tried to get that idea across to me especially about boys. He encouraged me to hold out for someone who is better than what I think I deserve, and to guard my heart. I think for teenagers, obviously, that's often how their hearts get broken and relationships can really turn bad. Obviously, I've used that idea in my life to look at boys and ask whether this person is somebody who my dad would think is worthy, who can guard my heart.

Murphy: I think one of the biggest ways that my dad has impacted me is just in watching my parents' marriage. And I know that so many of the good things that are in their marriage came from my grandparents. I really love how Grandpa is so intentional about honoring Grandma. And he even has a whole list of things that he loves about Grandma and that are special about her, and that's how he honors her. And I've seen that same attitude through my dad with my mom. And then because of that—of course, Dad honors his daughters as well and his son. Having two generations of marriages that have been very successful, encourages me to know that I have the tools to do what it takes to have a successful marriage someday.

Examples of Safety and Honor

As we mentioned in an earlier chapter, children have fewer and fewer examples of honor in their lives these days. They live in a world where the family unit is changing, divorce is commonplace, and solid marriages are more and more rare. Yes, there's a tragic shift in society that erodes a feeling of relational safety.

But as you learn to honor yourself and choose to value each

person in your family, a loving atmosphere of safe expression will grow. Families were intended for this kind of environment. We all need it!

Remember the question I asked my kids? "Is there anything you could do to make me stop loving you?" That's a safety-building question.

In single parent homes, this can be supplemented with healthy relationships in the extended family. But now that you see how important a sense of safety is for children, perhaps you see the damage that certain dating relationships can cause to your children, or grandchildren.

Guard your children's safe zones above all else!

> **AS YOU LEARN TO HONOR YOURSELF AND CHOOSE TO VALUE EACH PERSON IN YOUR FAMILY, A LOVING ATMOSPHERE OF SAFE EXPRESSION WILL GROW.**

Safety in Writing

Have you ever tried to play a board game without knowing the rules? It feels a bit strange, right? And the uncertainty is frustrating.

In the same way, it's essential for your kids to have a clear understanding of how your family operates. This also fosters a secure, safe family experience.

When our kids were all under ten years of age, Norma and I created a "contract." This was a simple list to help everyone understand some things about our family.

- Honor God and others
- Obey Mom and Dad
- No complaining
- Pick up your own stuff before you go to bed

All these areas involve honor and create a sense of safety. For example, when we stayed in hotels, our kids would love to jump on the beds. I would say, "Hey, I think that's dishonoring to the hotel."

"How?" they would ask.

"You're jumping on their bed. Do you have permission to do that? Have you asked the manager if you can jump on this bed?" So the three of them would walk down to the front desk and ask if they could jump on the bed. Every time they would come back and say, "Yes! They said we can jump on the bed!"

Come to think of it, I'm not totally sure they asked the manager! They were never gone very long . . .

In some ways, those were simpler times. Now, computers, phones, and social media present opportunities for families to have clear agreement on what is acceptable and what is not.

As the kids got older, we eventually added some more points and expanded the details in the contract. For example, we didn't allow dating until we saw certain qualities active in their lives. They had to be spiritually connected, love God, love others, love themselves, and demonstrate good boundaries.

The Pledge

A few years ago, on a drive to one of our favorite fishing spots, our son Greg suggested, "I think we ought to sign a pledge. You know, how we want our family to be—something we can pass down to generations."

Although he was forty-five at the time, Greg was pointing out something every child yearns for: safety through clear communication. A family pledge is a tangible way to honor your spouse, your kids, and generations to come. Imagine your great-

great-grandchildren reading your family pledge someday!

I'll share our pledge later in the book!

Truth in Safety

My wife is great at creating safe conversations with our kids. Instead of telling them, "You better not smoke!" she would often say, "By the way, let me know if you're ever thinking about smoking. I'd love to talk about it if you're ever curious, and we can smoke one together." Our kids used to say, "Dang, that takes all the fun out of it, Mom!"

Does that approach seem backwards to you? Well, think about the safety-building power of that invitation. Would your children be more willing to talk with you after a command . . . or an invitation?

As the kids were growing up, Norma would say to other parents, "Just really be careful that you don't react when your young kids come to you and say something like, 'I've been watching porn at my friend's house.' Your first reaction will be to explode, but that response could shut off communication."

Children will naturally confide in their parents, until doing so feels unsafe.

Lying is often a result of an unsafe environment. When you see a pattern of lies develop, that's not the time to lash out, it's time to look in the mirror and consider how to build a safer environment for those you love.

Just like my constant judgment of Norma shut a part of her off from me, the same happens in your children with over-criticism. You may believe harping on your kids will cause them to change, but if they don't feel honored and safe, they'll distance themselves from you.

Aunts, uncles, grandparents, and cousins can also help foster a safe, honoring environment. That's how a healthy family grows for many generations.

Safety and Faith

Intimate conversations with your kids only happen when they feel safe. I suppose another way of looking at safety is this: it's the absence of self-consciousness. When kids feel safe with you, they'll blurt out the most ridiculous, shocking, and beautiful statements—straight from their hearts.

> " CHILDREN WILL NATURALLY CONFIDE IN THEIR PARENTS, UNTIL DOING SO FEELS UNSAFE.

You'll be able to talk about relationships, dreams, careers, and even their faith. These conversations will only go deeper and deeper as trust develops.

When you create a safe environment for kids to ask honest questions about faith in Jesus Christ, authentic discipleship will happen in your family.

No matter how big a youth group is, or how good the ministry leader is, it comes down to creating a safe environment for them to ask really good questions at home. It's transformational.

True discipleship happens when you create a safe environment for people to freely express who they are.

At some point in the last few years, Norma and I asked all our kids this question: "Why did you decide to follow the teachings of Jesus and begin living what He taught?"

In various forms, each replied, "Because you lived it. I heard you talking about how you wanted to help people but couldn't afford it. I heard you pray, and we prayed as a family, and I watched

God deliver amazing answers to your prayers. The transparency made such an impact on me."

We simply lived our faith openly, and they saw the miracles God did in our family.

Safety grows within your children's hearts as you take responsibility for becoming what you want them to become. Kids learn best by example.

Freedom

Does your spouse feel safe to talk honestly?

Are your kids distancing themselves?

Are you trying to change them?

No matter how good or bad the level of communication is in your family, building a safe zone will set the stage for more open and truthful conversations.

Are you ready for those talks? Are you open to constructive feedback? Those conversations are a gift.

My family's not perfect. Roger and Kari, Greg and Erin, Michael and Amy, and all our wonderful grandkids aren't perfect. But we're safe to tell each other if we're "messing this up." And it feels so good to be a part of three generations who are committed to honoring each other.

4

THE DEADLY INFECTION

Most families carry a dangerous infection but have no idea how destructive this "relationship disease" can become.

You're probably a carrier of this disease and not even aware of it. Once infected, you can easily spread it to other family members.

This condition kills from the inside out. It damages your heart, mind, vital organs—and destroys relationships. I'm going to teach you how to spot this infection and take steps to be healthy.

Does this sound a bit dramatic? I'm as serious as a . . . well, let me continue.

As you read this, families, communities, and even countries are being decimated. Generations will be ruined by this disease, unless we step in.

Still think I'm being theatrical? If I could, I'd look you in the eye, clasp your hands in mine, and beg you to listen. I've lost kidneys and had a heart attack because of this deadly infection.

My son, Michael, even lost a rib and a kidney because I carried this poison.

The worst part: I had no idea. This disease blinds you from understanding the symptoms.

Symptoms

Frustration, disappointment, heartbreak, fear, criticism, unmet expectations, and constant worry are some of the symptoms— and causes.

So is bright-green skin.

You know, like The Incredible Hulk, the comic book character whose change in appearance was unmistakable when angered. The destructive infection I'm referring to is: anger.

I really wish that anger would be as obvious as green skin, so we could see it clearly and purge every drop from our lives.

But there are other ways to see anger in all its forms and be free from its ugliness. Ironically, we need to "honor" anger for the deadly infection it is, so we can guard ourselves and our family against it. The first step in ridding the infection is simply to recognize anger, in yourself and in your family members.

Although anger is natural, we're not designed to carry this emotion for long periods of time. Many people do. And many families pass anger through generations.

"In your anger do not sin," the apostle Paul wrote. "Do not let the sun go down while you are still angry" (Ephesians 4:26).

Jimmy's Anger

My favorite example of a young life transformed from anger to overwhelming victory is our family friend Jimmy.

He was an extremely traumatized child, abused by his alcoholic father. Jimmy grew up hating his dad for the beatings he and his family endured night after night. His worst memory was watching his dad beat his sweet mom.

As a young boy, unable to intervene, he acted out in disruptive ways. Lying on his back in the dust after another schoolyard scuffle, Jimmy looked up and saw something he'd never seen before. (We'll talk about this later.)

He could easily have been overcome by the anger, and the rest, so to speak, would be history: decades in prison for his crimes.

Anger, along with all of its reflections, can leave a person emotionally disabled. Everything potentially good about little Jimmy could have been killed, stolen, and destroyed.

Anger is the root of every form of negative human behavior. Today we see it in gang behavior, violence, racial hatred, and every war ever waged.

I watched anger creep into my life in my middle thirties to the point that I couldn't understand why I'd lost interest in spiritual matters. I was stuck, unable to break loose from the angry grip.

I've been learning over the years, that when we begin the process of reducing the level of anger towards anyone, we don't take the action for the sake of others. We do it to enjoy the blessing of obedience ourselves and to avoid the deadly poison of anger.

Honoring others motivates us to keep ourselves, and others, as anger-free as possible.

We'll follow the path Jimmy took to reduce anger so you can see the amazing miracle that began in that dusty field. I want you to see how he became athlete of the century in Oil City, Pennsylvania. How he became a hero for the people of his city, who built a school park in his honor.

I want you to understand the gift that was given to Jimmy, which brought amazing earning power. He was able to play professional football for the New England Patriots and invented an exercise machine that created tens of millions of dollars in sales.

Designed to Be Anger-Free

At a conference a few years ago, I heard Dr. Caroline Leaf, a neuroscientist from South Africa, explaining her studies of the brain. She even showed MRI scans of a brain from someone who did not love well at the moment. The image showed a cloud in the brain.

Halfway through her presentation she stopped and said, "You know, the brain was really only created to do one thing. And when the brain does it really well, you operate at your highest capacity. The brain was created to love."[2]

HONORING OTHERS MOTIVATES US TO KEEP OURSELVES, AND OTHERS, AS ANGER-FREE AS POSSIBLE.

This statement is fascinating, because we're told by Jesus that our very purpose is to love (see Matthew 22:37–39). When you're loving well and receiving love, your brain is functioning at its highest capacity. Although I'm no brain scientist, I do know that our brains control our bodies and the complex mix of chemicals designed to keep us healthy.

We're created to process anger, but not to carry it. If we allow layer after layer of frustration, disappointment, heartache, fearful thoughts, unmet expectations, and worry to build up, these emotions will erode our health—spirit, soul, and body.

Allowing anger to reside within us causes our vital organs

to reduce their efficiency. There is overwhelming evidence that suicides in all walks of life are directly linked to large amounts of stored anger within the heart.

All the doctors I've spoken with, and I've seen several, have told me that internalized anger, over a long period of time, causes over 85 percent of physical health problems.

Just as I would be careful to wash my hands, and even scrub them, after being around infectious situations, we must scrub anger from our souls on a daily basis. I'm not being cute here. The analogy is appropriate because unresolved anger is dangerous. And it permeates our being in unexpected ways.

Expecting More

Fear, frustration, envy, jealousy, worry, greed, rage, depression . . . these are all aspects of anger, and one of the root causes is often unmet expectations.

Does this surprise you?

Deep down, we all have unfulfilled hopes. Many of these are buried deep inside, perhaps from our childhood to present-day disappointments. I probably have a list of three or four pages of hopeful expectations about life. The unexpected twists and turns of life try to cross those hopes off our lists. Sometimes they succeed.

When expectations are dashed, we get angry. The level can range from irritated to raging. If we're not attuned to the presence of anger, we won't face it, and therefore can't deal with it. So the unresolved emotion gets added to the storehouse we carry inside.

As you read this book, be on the lookout for anger in your own heart and pay attention to the root causes—including unmet expectations.

Personally, I get really frustrated with little bitty stuff. I'm pretty good with the big things, but little disappointments really seem to get under my skin. When I began studying the subject of anger, I realized these frustrations pop up because they're based on unmet expectations—of all sizes.

Culture of Anger

Have you watched the television news lately?

Now that you're becoming aware of the destructive infection of anger, take another look at society's problems. Why are so many people yelling, protesting, and committing acts of violence? Why are kids turning away from their parents?

We live in a culture full of anger and disappointment.

The more I recognize the destructive power of anger, the more I realize it's the number one destroyer of everything good around the globe, in our families, and our own lives. Anger is behind the massive increase in evil in our world. Even nations carry anger toward other nations for generations.

In the United States, and other democracies, it seems all sides of the political spectrum have one thing in common: they are angry!

What can we do to turn the tide? Again, it all comes down to the power of a healthy family—for your life and for generations to come.

Try to imagine what life would be like on this earth if the majority of people were free from anger and alive with honor toward one another. Division, based on anger, in our society is ripening us for turmoil.

The answer is not found in more "programs." Well-meaning politicians have spent trillions, yet the problems grow. Political movements like communism and socialism have attempted to force harmony and only created more angry strife.

Family Is Not the Answer

Surprised by that statement? Well, most people already have some kind of family. What we really need, what you and I need, is a *healthy* family. The goal is to be free from all forms of unresolved anger!

Very few people have a healthy family. I grew up in a home filled with anger and was emotionally distant from my dad. As a child, I had no clue about the choices I could make to change my life and relationships.

I was sitting in my favorite chair recently and pondered for over an hour about all the people I've known whose bitterness divided them from friends and family. I also started counting the number of political groups that are fanning the flames of anger and division in our country and all over the world. And I could go on and on about the destructive behavior of Christ-followers who hate each other and do very little to live together in unity and love.

What's the answer to all this pain? Keep your heart free from anger.

Most people simply don't know how infected they are. The more we expect people, places, and things to bring us a good life, the more we tend toward disappointment, greed, jealousy, and the other emotions that lead us to misery. Almost all of society's evil acts ooze out of people who carry anger.

Missed Understandings

Years ago I was speaking at a conference in Hawaii, so Norma and I took our teenage kids with us.

We were staying at a friend's condo, which was near some outdoor shopping. "I've got some things to do," I told the family. "You guys walk down to the shops, and I'll meet you at four o'clock by the ice cream shop."

I finished up some phone calls and notes, put on my flip flops, and headed to the meeting place. Four o'clock came and went. Four-fifteen came and went. For some reason I thought they were playing a game and trying to lose me, as a joke. After twenty more minutes of waiting I went back to the condo. (Yes, this was before the age of cell phones, so we couldn't contact each other. And no, I didn't notice any dinosaurs.)

As I waited for Norma and the kids to return, I was stewing. I felt betrayed and disrespected, even imagining they didn't want to be with me. This was early in my discovery of how dangerous anger could be, and I still acted a lot like my father, who was very angry and verbally abusive.

ALMOST ALL OF SOCIETY'S EVIL ACTS OOZE OUT OF PEOPLE WHO CARRY ANGER.

When Norma and the kids finally arrived back at the condo and asked, "Where were you?" I blew up. "You weren't where we agreed to meet! I waited for over half an hour. I can't believe how selfish and inconsiderate you all are! What's the matter with you?"

After some cooling down, my son Greg asked me if I wanted to stay just like my father was. Translation: angry. That question always humbled me, but I'd given my family permission to ask hard questions.

When I finally calmed down and realized anger had gotten the best of me, I confessed to my family.

"I hate that I get angry and upset like this. Would you be willing to pray with me and ask God to break the cycle of anger?

I recognize it from my grandfather and my father. I want a whole new Smalley family. Could we do that?"

We gathered around the table and asked God to give us a new Smalley generation. That's exactly what we got . . . in time.

Roots of Disappointment

Why did I get so upset and blast my family with destructive words? At that moment I blamed them for the fact they missed our meeting time. But you're already smarter than I was back then—you know there was something deeper brewing in me.

The root issue was anger from being controlled or dishonored. Whether true or not, the very appearance of dishonor triggered anger inside me. Some of it can be traced back to my challenges in school, and the ridicule I endured, which I'll share in another chapter.

When our expectations aren't met, we're prone to anger. When two or three, or three hundred disappointments are stuffed inside, they fuel the fire of destructive anger.

Unmet expectations also cause stress. In today's society we attribute stress to busyness and hectic schedules. But I challenge you to look deep inside and ask God to show you where stress is really coming from. I didn't realize where my stress was coming from until I started looking for the root causes of my anger.

Identifying Expectations

Almost all anger comes from unmet expectations.

Take a moment and think about what you expect in life, or maybe, what you used to expect from life before you gave up hope . . .

- About yourself
- About your marriage
- About your kids
- About your family's future

When was the last time you really "lost it" in anger? Stop and think about the causes below the surface.

If you're a follower of Christ's teachings, ask the Holy Spirit to counsel you. Jesus said believers would receive power and help from the Holy Spirit, often referred to as our Helper or Counselor (see John 14:26).

Married to Expectations

Almost all anger toward your spouse comes from unmet expectations. Since we all have hopes and assumptions about life, we all need to recognize how this applies to our marriages. And boy-oh-boy, people have high expectations for marriage!

Just like my outburst in Hawaii, stored anger will distort our sense of reality—our sense of ourselves and our view of our mate.

For example, if your spouse makes purchasing decisions you don't agree with, you might believe it's just an innocent habit at first. If the pattern continues, despite discussions and possibly heated arguments, you might start believing the worst.

ALMOST ALL ANGER COMES FROM UNMET EXPECTATIONS.

You may believe your spouse doesn't respect you and is a selfish person. You may hide money, keep secrets, and even lie because of your anger. None of us hope for disappointment or pain in marriage. If we're ignorant about the deadly infection of anger, we're vulnerable.

Eventually, you might start believing you're married to the wrong person. The moment you start believing this way, you'll tune into signs that reinforce the belief (and ignore all the valuable qualities about your mate).

See how anger can snowball?

Feeding Frenzy

What do you and your spouse argue about? What topics or situations seem to trigger arguments that explode—seemingly for no reason?

The reasons are hidden in anger. All escalated arguments have nothing to do with the issue you're arguing about. Nothing.

Let me say that another way. Those particular talks that spark into verbal fireworks are never about the topic at hand. For example, angry arguments about money are never about money.

You're simply angry about one of your core fears. Core fears are defined by deeply unhappy experiences in your youth. My own two core fears are:

1. Fear of being controlled by people
2. Fear of being dishonored in front of people

One of the major crises in my life was failing the third grade. You can only imagine what was said to me and how I must've felt when I got the news. I would be held back—away from my friends for the rest of my life!

That terrible experience resulted in two deep core fears, and the slightest reminders used to bring me to intense anger almost immediately.

If Norma said anything that *sounded* controlling or

belittling, I used to go off. I even lost some very good friends because they stepped on my two core fears.

Almost all conflicts arise from these hot-buttons. That's the root problem—and it's your problem, too. For example, the subject of money triggers such a wide array of hidden fears and expectations: "Can I really trust my spouse?" "Is money the only thing keeping us together?"

So many thoughts, memories, and deep-seated reactions come directly out of our core fears.

For most adults, especially men, it's easier to express anger then the feelings behind our anger. But if you're not honest with yourself, how can you have an honest conversation with your mate?

If you don't get to the root issues of anger and fear, arguments will continue to escalate. A relationship full of hurtful arguments becomes an unsafe place. And whenever your marriage becomes an unsafe place, you won't want to be there anymore.

All four causes of divorce are based in anger:

1. Escalated arguments
2. Withdrawing
3. Belittling
4. Negative, false beliefs about your mate

More specifically, all four of these areas are rooted in unresolved anger. So how do we step into this minefield of emotion and bring harmony?

Detecting Anger

We can try to hide anger, but the signs are evident—if you know what to look for. Your mate's emotions will show themselves in actions. Your child's heart is going to reveal itself in behavior.

Keep watch for signs of anger with the same intensity as you look for signs of illness.

Body language can be an excellent indicator. An angry person, when approached, will usually turn away; when hugged they will tighten up.

Spontaneous playfulness and warmth are signs of a heart free from anger. I've had pillow fights with my kids that escalated into hilarious laughter and hugging, and I've had pillow fights that escalated into hitting. When that happened, I always wondered if I was the one who offended them, or somebody else?

Either way, there's an opportunity to help release toxic anger. We'll talk more about this in the next chapter.

Every one of my kids, and grandchildren, process anger differently. Some seem to never be angry, others react immediately and want to talk it out—and everything in between. Your child's heart is going to reveal itself in their behavior—how they think, what they say, and what they do is the reflection of their heart. So always be looking, learning, and valuing.

Provoked to Anger

As parents, we often provoke anger with criticism. It may seem as though we're pointing a child back to the right path, but if we aren't watchful for anger, we'll distance ourselves from our kids.

Remember, anger is a deadly infection. One of the secondary reasons I hugged and held hands with my kids was to see if they were mad at me. I was intentional about detecting and removing anger. If I sensed resistance, then I'd know someone had offended them. This emotion shows up as tightening muscles during a hug or pulling away their hands.

---
(2)

I will learn to keep my anger at the lowest level each day toward every family member or in any situation.

Unresolved anger will close a child's heart toward you as a parent. They won't be open to your words or your heart, and eventually, they won't want to be a part of your family.

That's why a sense of safety is so important in a healthy family. When you ask questions like, "How was school today?" a child who feels safe will be able to confide in you and process emotions.

One day Norma and I were driving to the airport and discussing an issue we disagreed about. I had my side, and she had hers. Normally, I would have been plotting my victory speech, crushing her perspective with my superior logic, and escalating into a fiery argument.

But I was learning about the destructive power of anger and simply chose to relax. Instead of winning, at the cost of safety and honor, my goal was to understand my wife. As we drove, I just listened to her for an hour and a half—her thoughts and feelings. I probably spoke a dozen words in ninety minutes. And you know what? We solved our disagreement along the way.

It's not acceptable to have one person feel like a loser, so we just win-win. We always come to a win-win, and it's always miraculous. Sometimes we stop and pray, "God give us wisdom here. Give us a suggestion."

That's the power of honor—honoring God and honoring your family.

Because you honor your spouse, your kids, or your grandkids, you want them to be free from the dangerous infection of anger . . . every single day.

Dealing with Past Anger

We all have some anger buried in our past. Yes, this storehouse must be emptied as well. The infection must go.

That's the subject of our next chapter. And it's a miracle.

5

THE MIRACLE

Athlete of the Century—that's an honor I never received, but my great friend Jimmy did, in Oil City, Pennsylvania. He broke dozens of football records and still holds a lot of them. There's even a park named after him! Being stocky and strong, Jim made the perfect running back, which even led to a career in the NFL.

His home life was anything but perfect, with an alcoholic father who beat him and his mother. Jim's anger fueled his very identity. Many top athletes thrive on the praise they receive in sports because they didn't get positive feedback at home.

Remember the little boy fighting on the playground in the previous chapter? That was little Jimmy. Now he's big Jim.

One day in high school, Jim was walking home from football practice. Opening the front door, he heard his mother screaming. He bolted up the stairs and caught his dad beating her. This wasn't an unusual occurrence, but this time Jim was ready, emotionally and physically, to do something about it.

"If you touch Mom again, I'll kill you. You aren't allowed to touch her ever, or my sisters and brothers, again. That's it!"

Seventeen years of rage exploded. Jim grabbed his father and threw him . . . out the second-story window.

No Release

Maybe the awning, which broke his fall, saved his dad's life. Or maybe it was because his dad was so drunk he flopped onto the grass without injury. But that wasn't enough for Jim.

He ran down the stairs, onto the lawn, grabbed his dad by the collar and repeated, "Did you hear me? You will not live!"

Jim could release some of the rage on the football field but could never get free from it. In fact, when I first met him, he couldn't even talk about his dad. Even in his forties, Jim was an imposing figure, and to be honest, I didn't want to press him too much on the subject.

> IF WE WANT TO TRULY ENJOY OUR LIVES, WE MUST EVEN HONOR THE PERSON WHO OFFENDED US AS SOMEONE GOD VALUES. HONOR IS THE REASON WE FORGIVE.

After three or four conversations, I knew it was time to help release the anger that had been poisoning him. I asked a shocking question.

We Need a Miracle

How do we free ourselves and our loved ones from the deadly poison of anger? It takes a miracle.

We must intentionally empty our anger on a daily basis

and give our family an opportunity to empty themselves of this infection. There's a word for this process, and you've heard it before. I'm talking about the miracle of *forgiveness*.

If forgiveness sounds like an impossible challenge, the alternative is much more difficult to live with. That's why I say unforgiveness is like drinking poison and hoping your offender gets sick!

Here's our third key to a healthy heart, and a healthy family.

I will learn every way possible to forgive my family members each day and seek forgiveness when I offend any one of them. I promise to help each family member remain in harmony, as much as I'm able.

We know how deadly unresolved anger can be. Forgiveness is the release valve! We'll explore several ways to get free from past anger and keep unforgiveness from taking hold in our families.

Honoring Others

There's obviously more to unforgiveness than meets the eye.

Jesus made His view quite clear: "Therefore, if you are offering your gift at the altar and there remember that your brother or sister has something against you, leave your gift there in front of the altar. First go and be reconciled to them; then come and offer your gift" (Matthew 5:23–24).

> **WHEN ANGER IS UNRESOLVED, YOUR HOME WON'T FEEL SAFE, AND WHEN SAFETY DOESN'T EXIST, YOUR FAMILY WON'T COMMUNICATE OPENLY.**

God isn't interested in our gifts if there's unresolved anger in the air.

We must honor the destructive power of anger, honor God's wisdom, and honor ourselves. If we want to truly enjoy our lives, we must even honor the person who offended us as someone God values. Honor is the reason we forgive.

People are so valuable they're worth taking the time to approach and say, "I think I've offended you. Please forgive me."

Your family is so valuable, you'll want them free of anger. You are so valuable to God and to your family, you need to be free of anger, too!

Remember what my grandson Michael shared about my dishonoring words? Well, he was angry. Here's more from him.

PROFESSIONAL FORGIVERS

"We're not getting out of this car until we work this out," I told Grandpa.

Sure, I told him that his comments about food were the opposite of honor. But deep down, I wanted this resolved. You know, there's kidding, and there are comments that keep hurting.

"Okay. Tell me how that makes you feel," he said.

"What I appreciate about our relationship is that I can be honest. But your words make me feel . . .

that my weight is stopping you from loving me. I don't feel any support, just criticism."

Grandpa apologized, of course. But I needed to be heard and to release the anger that was building up towards him. After that I was able to feel his support, and listen to him. He just wanted me to be healthy.

My parents, and Grandpa and Grandma, taught me how important it is to keep our hearts open and not carry anger around. We're constantly forgiving each other. I think it's because of the love and honor I have for my family. Forgiveness is just so much bigger than the problem, so much bigger than the conflict.

Of course it's hard to forgive somebody, but you do it out of love for them. You do it because you highly honor them and value them.

We're all professional forgivers now.

A Mirror

Forgive others who irritate you because they aren't perfect. Then turn your attention to your own heart. Again, there's certainly a connection between forgiveness and relationships—including our relationship with God, who loves us and wants the best for us.

"But if you do not forgive others their sins, your Father will not forgive your sins" (Matthew 6:15). Wow! That's pretty clear, isn't it?

Think about this truth in the context of your family. If

there's resentment in your family, no one is truly happy. When anger is unresolved, your home won't feel safe; and when safety doesn't exist, your family won't communicate openly.

Understand that when you're irritated by others, often these frustrations are reflections of your own immaturity or blind spots caused by "logs" in your eyes. You can choose to use those irritations to seek your own growth, instead of reacting or blaming others.

We need to look in the mirror and search for logs of unforgiveness in our eyes. And we need to be open to hear about those logs from our family, too.

Open Invitation

My daughter Kari had an unusually serious look on her face. She was about twelve years old and already had a good sense of the importance of family harmony. She also took me up on my invitation to help me be a better parent, as did all our kids.

"Dad, I want you to understand something important that's happening in our family, and I'm not sure you really see it."

She had my full attention.

"Okay," she said, "imagine you're speaking at a high school and they locked all the doors in the auditorium. Instead of sharing a message, you start criticizing the students for their behavior, calling them out individually. How do you think those kids would react to your speech?"

"They wouldn't like it at all! That would be terrible!" I answered curiously.

"But the problem is, Dad, they can't get out because the doors are all locked. And so, can you imagine the noise that's going to start? You're going to have a hard time speaking over the noise of the students yelling and throwing things at you."

"Yeah, I really get it," I said.

Kari took a deep breath and looked me in the eye. "I'm sure you're not aware of this, but this is how you treat my little brother Michael."

"What do you mean this is how I treat Michael?"

"You're on his case all the time," she said. "He's a captive audience because you can make him sit there, and then you start going over one thing after another. I think you've probably given him enough criticism to last his lifetime. I mean I think you should really consider stopping it all together . . . no more."

> ISN'T IT AMAZING HOW CLEARLY WE SEE THE FAULTS OF OTHERS AND HOW BLIND WE CAN BE TO OUR OWN?

After I regained my composure, I went to Michael and asked him, "Do you think I criticize you a lot?"

"That's the understatement of the century. Yes, you do, Dad," he said with a mix of relief and anger, and went on to list several examples.

One of the examples Michael reminded me of was how I often criticized him at the breakfast table. When he ate cereal, milk would always drip down his chin. (It's funny how years later, I happened to walk by a mirror after eating breakfast and saw milk on my chin.)

And funny that I wrote much of this book while staying in his home, under the care of him and his family! I'll share more about this later.

Isn't it amazing how clearly we see the faults of others and how blind we can be to our own?

Generations of Forgiveness

I was angry with myself, so I got angry at others, including my kids. Anger was in the air, and I wasn't aware of it. I had become accustomed to it as a child! Once I saw that log in my eye, I apologized to Kari and Michael, and they forgave me.

This is a pretty tame example, but you can see how unresolved anger can infect a family. Thankfully, my young daughter felt safe enough to bring up the issue. Addressing it, and releasing the hurt, brought us closer together.

Five Steps to Forgiveness

We all need some guidance in the process of forgiveness. When you sense anger in yourself, or in a family member, consider these five steps:

1. Be gentle. Remember you probably have milk on your face and logs in your eyes.
2. Be open to learn, to increase your understanding of the person and the situation.
3. Admit wrongs. Don't excuse or bury the truth about how you've hurt others.
4. Seek forgiveness with no expectations. Allow the other person to process their feelings.
5. Once you've talked things out, hold hands or hug, to check in on their heart. Be sensitive to how open they are to you.

Why wait a single day to forgive or to allow a family member the opportunity to forgive you?

I'm personally acquainted with the crushing weight of unforgiveness. I know the process of releasing anger can be difficult, and I realize that your offenders might not be safe people to talk to or be around. But you can still forgive. You must forgive.

It's possible.

Releasing My Anger

There was a time in my life when hatred was a constant companion. Early in my career, I was deeply hurt by people I trusted.

I was bitter. I was vengeful. I didn't like God anymore, and I didn't like myself. My family was obviously affected by this season of life, too.

Time doesn't heal all wounds. For two years I prayed, "God, please give me the gift of forgiveness." But anger seethed inside of me, and revenge dominated my thoughts. I was tormented and desperate.

The answer came in a surprising way. I was working in a church at that time, and one of the men asked me, "Would you read this article about forgiveness?"

I was shocked—*How did he know I needed to forgive?*

Then he added, "I need to forgive someone, but I need help. I'm sure you're really good at this—would you read this article and meet with me?" Whew! I put my best counselor face back on and told him I'd be glad to help.

I devoured the article right away. Although the advice seemed a bit strange, I knew those words were a gift from God.

Another Path

I blocked out some time by myself in a quiet room. The article said to imagine there were two other people in the room: Jesus and the person you hate.

Yes, I'm completely serious. I was desperate for a way to release my anger. I even arranged three chairs to help visualize the scene.

I began by saying, out loud, every way this person had offended and hurt me. Even though I hadn't been around this person in more than two years, the memories were vivid. So I declared the first offense: *He wrongly accused me and dishonored me in front of the entire group.*

I vented every detail and got pretty loud in the process. Then I imagined Jesus saying to the man who offended me, "Do you understand?" And saw the offender saying, "Yes."

TIME DOESN'T HEAL ALL WOUNDS— FORGIVENESS DOES.

Then I pictured Jesus turning to me and asking, "Gary, would you forgive him?"

I paused and held my breath for a long time before whispering, "Yes, I forgive him." As those words filled the air, I chose to erase that particular hurt from my life.

For three hours I stayed in that room and detailed every offense I could think of. I prayed. I fell to my knees and cried. I screamed. After each offense was aired, and forgiven, I pictured Jesus asking me, "Now, where did you offend him like he offended you?"

Honestly, listing my offenses was as difficult as forgiving the other person. After all, I was the one who was wronged—there was no debate about that.

After a few minutes of internal wrestling, I saw some logs in my eyes. I confessed those to my Lord and imagined my offender was in the room with us.

"I'm a mess because I can't forgive!"

Nothing

As I rearranged the furniture, I felt pretty silly. Nothing had happened. I was really disappointed. *I put my whole heart into this, not to mention three hours, and I don't feel any different.*

Three weeks later, Gary Smalley woke up a free man. I felt so excited about life, and I was totally free of any anger towards that person. Then I started realizing, little by little, that my whole view of life was changing.

I had a brand new compassion for people—especially those unhappy in their marriages. Somehow, I was able to identify deeply with the pain in families of divorce. In my gut, I suddenly understood how people felt while being hurt and abused.

And I had a different kind of emotional energy . . . aimed at the destructive power of anger and unforgiveness.

This experience happened before I entered my calling to help marriages and families. Looking back, it's clear that forgiveness was the doorway to my ministry—and the key to leading my own family.

Imagine what wondrous possibilities and new adventures await you and your family, when you learn to forgive!

Let's keep going.

Hindsight and Forgiveness

Time doesn't heal all wounds—forgiveness does.

As the days and weeks passed, I actually started thanking God for allowing that hurtful situation to happen. Had I not felt the pain, I wouldn't have a tender heart toward my family and all the families of the world.

I was actually grateful for this offender and even thankful for the pain. "And we know that in all things God works for the good of those who love him, who have been called according to his purpose" (Romans 8:28). The apostle Paul wrote those words and described the suffering so many of us experience in life and how God can create goodness from it.

One good gift God gave me through this experience was a mega-dose of high emotional intelligence. Before I was able to forgive this man, I had a fair amount of intellectual intelligence but not emotional intelligence. Norma and my kids will testify to this fact.

I received a gracious gift from God through the pain—a passion for helping couples and families in their troubled relationships.

Forgiveness is a miracle. We need God's help in order to forgive.

Forgiveness also brings miracles. The fact that I was able to write this book, or any book, is a miracle of forgiveness. Maybe it's a miracle that you're reading this book!

Keep asking God to help you along the way.

Final Forgiveness

We don't always have the opportunity to confront those we've offended, or seek forgiveness from those who have hurt us. Some people may not be safe to be around, they may be in prison, or they may have passed into eternity.

"But my father is dead. How can I forgive him?" I hear this question a lot.

You just do it. The same way I described above—or your own version. With any process you choose, ask for God's help. He invented forgiveness.

As you recognize the danger of unresolved anger and the beautiful power of forgiveness, you'll face two different challenges. First, releasing past anger, which we just described, and second, maintaining an atmosphere of forgiveness in your heart and with your family.

LUV Talk

Anger likes to show up in disagreements. In fact, escalating arguments are a sure sign of unresolved anger. Most people, myself included, are naturals at adding fuel to the fire. But we need to learn how to quench the anger before anyone gets burned.

Let me remind you why this is so important. Anger is a deadly infection. We're not designed to carry this emotion around inside us, and we don't have to!

One of the ways to process anger is to try a completely new way to deal with issues together. I call this LUV talk.

Admit it. You can feel stress build in a conversation gone wrong. You feel your blood pressure rise and your brain cells start to explode. Your chest tightens and your ears begin to close. You're about to roll your eyes, sigh, yell, or throw your best sarcastic bomb.

We all know how this will end.

Instead of venting or reacting, take these signs as an invitation to change course. Yes, this can be extremely difficult when you feel frustrated or attacked. That's where LUV talk comes in.

When you detect anger . . .

- **L**isten
- **U**nderstand
- **V**alidate

That's LUV!

Disagreements are a gift—an opportunity for greater love and harmony. If you don't believe me now, you will. Let's give this a try.

LISTEN

I love talking to the staff at drive-through restaurants. Sure, I usually try to spark some friendly conversation, but you know what I love most about the experience? The listening.

The crew members don't question my feelings or try to talk me out of what I want. They simply listen and usually repeat what I said to make sure they heard me correctly.

"Welcome. What would you like today?"

It feels great to be heard. But often at home we're afraid to offer an opinion, a request, or a heartfelt desire without being judged or dismissed. There's a time for discussion and opinion, but that time is after real listening happens.

"And hold the lettuce, tomato, and onion, please . . ."

"But those vegetables are healthy! What's the matter with you? When was the last time you had a salad? I'm changing your order to a large salad. Please pay at the first window," a voice crackles through the speaker.

Does this remind you of discussions with your mate?

Listening is so easy, yet we rarely do it well. Take a deep breath and really absorb what the other person is saying. By the way, taking slow, deep breaths is a wonderful alternative to interrupting. No matter the topic, try to hear the needs and feelings being expressed. That's your only job: listening.

UNDERSTAND

Remember, the goal is to listen well, so you can understand the needs and feelings of the other person. It's okay to ask questions in order to understand. (Just not the "How many burgers did you eat this week?" kind of questions.)

You can't talk and listen at the same time, but the "understand" phase of LUV talk is an opportunity to ask thoughtful questions.

"Can you tell me more about that time?"

"Help me understand why you feel that way, will you?"

> VALIDATION MEANS YOU NOT ONLY UNDERSTAND THE OTHER PERSON'S FEELINGS AND THOUGHTS, YOU APPRECIATE AND HONOR THEM.

Agreement is optional. It's possible to understand and not agree, but the goal here is to simply understand and give the other person the honor of being understood.

VALIDATE

Value what your spouse has to say—no matter what. The same goes for your children, extended family, and friends.

Validation is a cousin to "value." Once you understand, instead of offering opinion or judgment, simply express appreciation for their perspective. Validation means you not only understand the other person's feelings and thoughts, you appreciate and honor them.

One way to really drive this home is to switch roles in the discussion.

"If I'm hearing you correctly, onions upset your stomach, and that's why you don't want them. I'm sorry I got on your case about onions."

Value what your spouse or child feels. Let them experience

being understood and valued for their perspective. Validation means you not only understand the other person's feelings, you honor them and create a priceless sense of safety—an essential part of a healthy family.

This is LUV talk, with three simple components. The most important step is the first step: stop to listen. Really listen.

From the Heart

The mistake many parents make is they force their kids to go through the motions of forgiveness. "You go and apologize right now for what you did!"

The problem is, their kids don't actually feel the need to forgive. They have no interest in doing it, so they're actually not learning about forgiveness. True apologies and real forgiveness come from a desire to honor. Healthy families understand the value of each member, know the destructive power of anger, and want to reconcile.

As you teach and demonstrate honor for each other, a child who mistreats his sibling will soon soften his heart, feel the pain he's inflicted, and seek forgiveness.

Distance

When our kids were young, I traveled a lot. I'd often arrive home from a long trip and receive a cold reaction from my son Greg, who was in junior high at the time.

He was so upset with me because of my absences, he'd ignore me, sometimes for an entire day—no hugging, no "great to have you back, Dad." He was full-on angry: *You were gone again; I don't like that. I wish you wouldn't leave.*

I tried to explain to him how terrible I felt about being gone, but nothing I said seemed to help.

One day I sat him down and said, "Tell me how you would feel if this happened to you. Let's pretend you're on a basketball team, and let's say you're a good player in practice. But when the games are played, the coach leaves you on the bench and doesn't play you. How would you feel?"

"I'd be really upset," he answered.

"You probably don't realize this, but that's how I feel about you ignoring me when I come home from a trip."

"What do you mean I treat you like that? I don't do that!"

"Yes, you do. You ignore me and leave me on the bench. You don't even notice me for hours sometimes." And I continued, "It really hurts me because one of my three kids is ignoring me. So that's how I feel."

I could see him soften as he listened. Greg took a deep breath and said, "Dad, I didn't really understand how that felt. I'm sorry."

The next time I was leaving for a trip, Norma and the kids were all saying goodbye and hugging me. Greg grinned and chimed in, "Have a great trip, Dad. But just remember, when you get home, I'm going to ignore you." We had a moment of understanding and laughter—and forgiveness.

What really fascinated me was how he remembered my story. My word picture connected with his emotions. By the way, he never rejected me again when I returned home after a trip.

We listened to each other, we understood each other's perspective, and we validated each other's feelings. Honor was strengthened, we both felt safe to express emotions, and anger was released. LUV talk with an eleven-year-old might sound a little different than LUV talk with a forty-year-old, but the goal of forgiveness is the same.

Live Forgiving

Pay attention to stress. Stress is a symptom of anger and an opportunity to choose forgiveness.

When I notice myself getting riled up inside about what someone did, I try to catch myself and forgive the person immediately. "Lord, thank you for revealing that to me. You're right, I am angry, and I'm holding onto it. So I forgive that person right now."

THE POINT IS TO DEVELOP AN INTERNAL ALARM SYSTEM TO DETECT UNFORGIVENESS AND REMOVE IT—FAST!

When I forgive people, it helps for me to say, "Smalley, you've done similar things to other people. You're a flawed yellow diamond, and so are they."

The point is to develop an internal alarm system to detect unforgiveness and remove it—fast! Here's a story from Norma.

INSTANT FORGIVENESS

I like to fiddle around in the garden, but I don't like spiders! My kids are astounded at how fast I can move to get a spider off my arm. Maybe you can relate. When I see one of those creepy crawlies on my skin, I'm instantly transformed into a ninja—zipping the spider off with lightning speed.

This is how we need to react to anger and unforgiveness; the moment we feel it, we swat it away like a poisonous spider. Be a ninja-zapper! And when we see an anger-spider trying to crawl on our spouse or kids, we react the same way.

With practice, you'll see the benefits of quick forgiveness. *But Norma*, I hear you thinking, *I'm right and he's wrong. He needs to sweat it out a little bit and feel some pain!*

Well, you may be right, but should either of you carry the poison of anger around for one minute longer than necessary?

There's been many a time when Gary and I were upset with each other—at 10:00 p. m. *I'm tired and don't want to seek forgiveness.* I think to myself, *the sun's already set, so I'll wait until tomorrow!*

But I've learned, the hard way, I'd rather be tired than tired and angry. Why carry an ounce of stress, when we can be free? I've also learned to honor my husband by resolving anger *before* we turn out the lights.

Darkness

I was living in darkness before I forgave the person who betrayed me.

Anger is a poison that causes blindness—not in the person you're angry towards, but in you!

Listen to the apostle John, "Anyone who claims to be in the light but hates a brother or sister is still in the darkness. Anyone who loves their brother and sister lives in the light, and there is nothing in them to make them stumble. But anyone who hates a brother or sister is in the darkness and walks around in the darkness. They do not know where they are going, because the darkness has blinded them" (1 John 2:9–11).

Just like my life's calling was made clear to me after I forgave and accepted forgiveness, you can have new light and direction, too—if you'll release your anger. This includes anger you might be holding toward yourself.

Questioning Jim

After a few counseling sessions with Jim, it was clear he was carrying tons of anger toward his father. Yes, throwing him out the window eliminated the physical abuse, but the infection of anger was still spreading.

I wasn't sure how to ask the question, but I knew it was time. Besides, I was nowhere near a window . . .

"How much were you wrong towards your dad, and how much was your dad wrong?"

"Are you kidding, Gary?" Jim roared. "This man was all wrong!"

I listened to him rant for a few minutes, and then reminded him that none of us is perfect. No matter how horrible the other person in a relationship may be, we all have some logs in our eyes.

"Okay. My dad was 97 percent wrong, and I was 3 percent," Jim said. "I did some mean things to him."

"You don't have to really do anything with the 97 percent except forgive," I explained, and shared my own story of forgiveness. "Now you need to focus on the 3 percent—you need to focus on your part in the relationship." He understood what I meant.

The next evening, Jim drove several hours to his dad's

house. "Hey, Dad, can we take a walk?" His dad, who was also a big man, was pretty surprised to see Jim but immediately agreed.

"Dad, I've been thinking a lot about our relationship. I really caused you a lot of pain when I was growing up and said a lot of things that were really unloving. So . . . I just wanted to ask you . . . if you could find it in your heart to forgive me."

"Jimmy, that was a long time ago," his dad finally said. "You don't even have to say this."

But Jim replied, "No, Dad, it's really important for me. It would mean a lot if you could just say, 'I forgive you, Son.'"

"Yeah, I forgive you, Jimmy."

It was late, so Jim decided to spend the night there. The mood was a bit awkward, but Jim had a deep satisfaction that he finally owned the 3 percent.

About 2:00 a. m., his dad came into the room, woke him up, and whispered, "Can I talk to you?"

In a flood of tears, Jim's dad said, "I'm the one who needs to know God like you do. I haven't lived a good life. And I did a lot of terrible things to you . . . and your brothers and sisters . . . and your mom, especially. And I need to know—how did you get to know God?"

So Jim led his dad to Christ. They became best friends. His dad lived ten more years, many of those living with Jim's family.

Honoring Yourself

I've met people who were pretty good at forgiving everyone—except themselves.

We all have blind spots and logs in our eyes. I'm convinced that part of the process of removing the log from our own eyes is forgiving ourselves.

It's humbling to confront our own weaknesses, and the

weakness of those around us. But we can follow Jesus' command to love others as we love ourselves. This means forgiving ourselves.

Forgiveness is love in action. No person can maintain a perfect life, and we're all capable of offending others. It's like the old saying, "Please be patient with me, God's not finished with me yet."

God's not finished with you, but He's willing to forgive you. If you want peace and love in your family, you must rid your soul of anger—including anger toward yourself.

Before we move on to the next chapter, I invite you to receive the forgiveness God has for you . . . right now.

Remember, He invented forgiveness for the very purpose of giving it to us. Accept this astounding gift, and honor the Giver by forgiving yourself.

This is the way from darkness to light—for you and your family.

6

DISCOVERING HIDDEN TREASURE

I've written a lot of books and had the privilege of helping many families. I've spoken at conferences all over the world. My three national TV shows allowed me to partner with celebrity families: Dick Clark, John Tesh and Connie Sellecca, Frank Gifford and Kathy Lee Gifford.

But I'm convinced that none of those opportunities would have happened if I hadn't learned to forgive. Do you believe me? Okay, let's go a step further.

Those blessings and many others, including the miracle of forgiveness, would not have occurred if I hadn't gone through some very painful situations. Growing up I was deeply hurt by my father, and early in my career I was betrayed by my employer. The pain I endured in those experiences actually worked great things in my life.

Are you still with me?

As a school kid, I was academically challenged. Teachers actually told me I was stupid, not just once but on several occasions. I failed the third grade. Being held back in school was especially rough because all my friends went on to the fourth grade, and they didn't let me forget it.

EACH AND EVERY ONE OF MY PERSONAL HEARTACHES HAS BLESSED ME WITH MANY TREASURES.

The message was clear: Gary Smalley was inferior. I believed that message and carried shame and uncertainty with me through high school, college, and into my career. So how in the world did a guy like me end up writing so many books? Did I get hit by lightning and receive an IQ boost? Not exactly.

One of many shifts occurred in me when I was doing research on one of my first books. I was quite intimidated by the process but discovered that the most popular books and training manuals are intentionally written on a sixth-grade level!

There I was, afraid and irritated because of my academic limitations for all these years. God exposed the truth—He had actually prepared me to reach the largest number of families possible because I had the ability to share helpful truths in a way that people could relate to!

Yes, I'm a simple man and thankful for it.

An Awesome Gift from God

Suddenly I was thrilled to have the ability to write and teach on simple terms. This revelation allowed me to let go of the embarrassment and anger I'd held onto since third grade . . . (both times!).

Being able to make peace with my past, and embrace my God-given personality and academic ability, was a defining moment for me. Instead of trying to be someone else, which was exhausting, I started to enjoy being myself. I began to see my past differently. I was able to thank God for how He had made me—and understand why I struggled in school.

I'll expand this idea more in a later chapter, but there's something about me that most people don't know. I highly honor all of my shortcomings, my miserable trials, everything that makes me angry, and all negative things that happen to me. Each and every one of my personal heartaches has blessed me with many treasures.

It's so hard to stay angry at anything that greatly benefits you. Here is a short list of how God has blessed me and rewarded me for things that initially made me angry!

- My sixth-grade writing "limitation" actually made me a better communicator.
- Being deeply hurt by a former boss made me emotionally intelligent and compassionate. I also learned about the miracle of forgiveness, which allowed me to help countless others experience the same freedom.
- Once I experienced this miracle, I could see exciting new ways to help couples and was able to dream God's dream for me.
- I learned that people, places, and things never make a person happy. God alone is my source of life, joy, peace, energy, and hope!

I used to be terrified of reading in front of people. As a young man, I was asked to read a section of the Old Testament in front of 300 college students and I completely stumbled. I was so nervous another student had to step in and finish reading. It was a mortifying trial.

My first job after graduating from seminary was at a small church, and I occasionally spoke during the service. I couldn't even brush my teeth on Sunday morning if I was going to preach, because of the nausea. I just knew I was going to fail in ministry.

I found comfort in the realization that God only gives His grace to the humble (see Proverbs 3:34 and James 4:6). *If I mess up, I get humbled. I get more of God's grace!* So when I started going on television, including talk shows like Oprah, I'd say to myself, *Well, if I'm going to be nationally humiliated, I'll have massive grace given to me!*

I knew God could turn my bad experiences into good for me, for my family, and, prayerfully, to help other people.

Diving Deep

Like diamonds, some of the most prized riches come from deep dark places.

For thousands of years people have been digging and diving into scary places, to find rare treasures. At first glance, these riches may look and feel quite unattractive. For instance, have you ever seen an oyster? I mean, it's not a pretty shell.

I've been to plenty of jewelry stores in my life, and I've never seen oysters for sale there. Divers risk their lives by swimming into the murky water, only to emerge with lumpy, gray chunks of ugliness.

But the pearls inside can be priceless.

Pearls begin as an irritation from an outside source. A grain of sand or other small particle gets stuck inside the shell of an oyster, and the refining process begins. Over many months, the speck of dirt becomes covered in layer upon layer of minerals, and is transformed into a beautiful gemstone.[3]

Sure, the pearl is beautiful, but it's found at the bottom of the ocean, inside a dirty oyster-shell, and surrounded by slimy goo. And there it waits—one of the least likely places on earth to look for a gem.

Once you take the risk to find the oyster, you have to work to uncover the treasure. Sometimes there's a lot of gross, messy stuff to sort through before the pearl is found.

Unimaginable good is often hidden inside ugliness. The same principle applies to the deep, dark places of our lives. But it takes faith, believing that what God said is true, to relate this truth to the ugly oysters in our past.

Paul reminds us, "Now to him who is able to do immeasurably more than all we ask or imagine, according to his power that is at work within us, to him be glory in the church and in Christ Jesus throughout all generations, for ever and ever! Amen" (Ephesians 3:20–21).

There's power at work within us—power to turn bad into good. I don't believe God put the pain or irritation in your past, but He's covering the experience with beauty. He's turning those specks of dirt into valuable treasures, layer by layer.

Don't you want to discover the pearls in your past?

Treasure Hunting

Getting fired from my job, where my colleagues and I were betrayed, was one of the greatest experiences that ever happened to me. I sure didn't realize it at the time, but Norma saw the good in it, and so did God.

It's unnatural for us to look for the good in the bad. Who would imagine a shimmering pearl could be formed in a slimy oyster? Like hunting for sunken treasure, you won't discover pearls unless you get in the water. The more you treasure hunt, the more good you can find. In the process, you'll also discover forgiveness and peace. Real freedom comes when you start recognizing how you've actually benefitted from the painful experience.

In high school, my girlfriend broke up with me. I was devastated for weeks. Then a friend said to me, "God protected you from her. If she's going to treat you like that before you're married, imagine what she'd be like after!"

Weeks later, she actually tried to get back together with me. "No, I'm sorry. That was too painful," I told her. This story is funny now, but at the time I thought my whole world was falling apart.

One time, after speaking about this subject in Texas, a teenage girl walked up to Norma and me and told us about some intense experiences she had as a child in foster care. She was miserable about her life. As I tried to explain treasure hunting to her, she finally paused and looked right at me.

"You know what? I think you're crazier than I am," she said. We had a good laugh, but I think she was starting to believe.

Here's what I'm asking you to do: Just open yourself to the possibility that there's treasure in the pain you've been carrying around. Will you do that?

Open an Oyster Shell with a Pen

Here's a simple step of faith. Get a pen and paper and write down some ugly oysters in your life. Why write these down? It's helpful to identify the experience and really stare it down so we can be honest about the pain.

Start by writing down a little oyster-experience. Perhaps write down a hurtful experience from the past week or a conflict at work. Yes, these oysters can be hard to open. Be patient, keep digging and keep writing. Here are a few suggestions for treasure hunting:

- Know that there's a pearl inside the ugly oyster. That's the basis for treasure hunting. Why bother to look if you don't believe? One of the main themes of Scripture, including Matthew 5:10–12, is how God can turn bad into good. The good is in there.
- Pay attention to what good things are happening in you. And take note of the good things happening around you because of the situation. Is your compassion for others increasing? What a treasure! Ask the Holy Spirit to show you the pearls. He is the Wonderful Counselor. Take time to quiet your mind and listen to Him.
- Look back on past trials and remind yourself of the good that came from the bad.
- Keep a list of the benefits. In other words, pay attention and write down the treasures that appear from the mess.

I'm actually hunting for pearls as I write this book! The health challenges I've experienced in recent months have been beyond difficult. But I've become closer to my kids and grandkids in the process.

Throughout the pain, my determination to help you and your family with these words has only increased. The wonderful stories I'll share in later chapters would not have happened without this trial.

I've learned that Norma and I can still grow. And my family has seen how "older" people can continue to increase in love and honor. Most of all, I've experienced overflowing love and honor from every one of them.

LOOK BACK ON PAST TRIALS AND REMIND YOURSELF OF THE GOOD THAT CAME FROM THE BAD.

Trust this "old" person; there are hidden treasures in your painful circumstances.

Hidden Pain

Many years ago, Norma and I were counseling the wife of a professional athlete. She was a mom of a two-year-old, and motherhood was troubling for her. Their little girl cried a lot and seemed to be very high-maintenance.

Her husband was concerned as well. He saw his wife becoming increasingly strict and acting out in anger towards their child.

"I've got to get help because I'm a mess," she confessed. "And I'm hurting my daughter, I know it!"

We asked her to tell us a little bit about her life and how she grew up. On a surface level, she was quite beautiful. But her childhood was extremely painful. Certain male family members abused her, sexually, and demeaned her value. She was repeatedly told that her only purpose in life was to offer pleasure for men.

That's so wrong and so evil. It's even more tragic because

so many women experience the same abuse.

Somehow she endured the emotional and physical pain and was now happily married to a caring husband who didn't understand the impact of her past hurts. She felt guilty and angry.

I asked, "Would you really like to be healed of this?"

"Yes," she answered.

So we treasure hunted for several weeks, which also involved releasing anger with forgiveness. We came to a place where she recognized something positive from her pain: She possessed a unique sensitivity and compassion for other girls who were abused.

"I can walk down the street in a city, and sense the vibes of a girl who's being sexually abused. I can literally feel it. I never realized this was a gift!" she said with a look of surprise and joy. I wish you could have seen her countenance change then and there, as she saw the pearl in her past and the clarity of purpose it gave her.

Soon after she discovered this pearl, she started volunteering in shelters that help victims of violence and other forms of abuse. Her conversations often mirrored this one:

"Tell me your story," she would say.

The girl would cry and tell this woman about her life and the hurt she suffered.

"I understand what you've been through and what you're going through."

The girl would look straight at her and with an angry tone, say, "There's no way you could understand."

This brave woman would share a little of her own story. The girls were amazed, "Really? That happened to you? But you seem so happy, and you're so beautiful. How is that possible?"

And then she began treasure hunting with them, for as long

as it took, to find the hidden pearls. This brave woman discovered how God wanted to overcome evil with good—in her heart and through her life! "And we know that in all things God works for the good of those who love him, who have been called according to his purpose" (Romans 8:28).

The more my friend shared her unexpected treasure with others, the more thankful and fulfilled she became. This healing also brought a new level of harmony to her marriage and to her relationship with her daughter. She and her family are living examples of God's goodness and His ability to turn pain into pearls.

> THERE ARE ALWAYS GREAT BLESSINGS AND SPIRITUAL TREASURES HIDDEN WITHIN EACH AND EVERY TRIAL OR EMOTIONAL HARDSHIP.

Jim's Pearls

You already know some of Jim's story, the abuse he suffered, and the anger he carried. As a teenager, he was forced to work in his dad's carpet cleaning business. This meant long nights and little sleep.

Jim would doze off in school, which resulted in poor grades and bad relations with teachers. He failed the fifth grade and was held back, earning the nicknames of "stupid," "dummy," and "idiot" from the other kids. The build-up of anger expressed itself in frequent fights with classmates.

One day after a particularly brutal schoolyard battle, a teacher appeared and picked up the ten-year-old from the dusty playground. This teacher looked Jimmy in the eyes and promised to help nurture the natural talent he saw.

"Will you let me help you?" the teacher asked Jimmy.

He promised Jimmy that he would help him in three areas

of his life. There would be crowds of people cheering him on—as a track, wrestling, and football star. Had Jimmy not been acting out of his rage, this teacher may never have stepped in.

Jim broke school records in track, wrestling, and football. He still holds many of those records five decades later as Athlete of the Century in that Pennsylvania town. And he played professional football in the NFL.

The high emotional intelligence Jim developed was a pearl that helped him earn millions and allowed him to help many other people. Walking down Main Street with Jim, you won't go far without being interrupted by friends and grateful citizens.

His story could have become the same tragic tale as the millions of criminals living behind bars. It's so sad to see all of the prisoners who have lost their way in the blindness of uncontrollable anger.

There's a better way to live. There's more to life than meets the eye.

Teaching Treasure Hunting

Treasure hunting doesn't come naturally to most people. That's why we need to teach this skill to our family and make it part of our legacy: *Son, do you see this good thing in my life? Let me tell you why this happened. Let me share the real story behind what you see here today . . .*

My children know all about my childhood and how God taught me to honor, to deal with anger, and to forgive. Norma and I have both encouraged our kids, and grandkids, to see the value in their trials.

We listen to each other's hurts. We understand their pain, and we validate each other's feelings.

When the time is right, we suit up and go treasure hunting.

$$\circledbullet{4}$$

I will take personal responsibility to find the pearls and God's blessings from each and every trial I face.

Treasure hunting is a way of finding as many pearls, or blessings from God, that you can find in all your trials, frustrations, irritations, and memories of wounded feelings. The rich discoveries will lower your anger level and will increase your honor levels.

For some reason it seems natural to hold on to past hurts: *My dad or mom did these things to me while growing up. My boyfriend or girlfriend did horrible things to me. My boss ruined my life. I lived in horrible conditions growing up or moved into terrible situations* . . . and so on.

These are all worthy of treasure hunting, and forgiving, so we can move on with new freedom and opened hearts. Use everything that's happened to you to have an even better life!

I know it isn't easy. But there are always great blessings and spiritual treasures hidden within each and every trial or emotional hardship. We can find them as we ask God to reveal them to us.

This concept is profound, but children can grasp it easily, as my granddaughters, Hannah Gibson and Murphy Smalley, and grandson, Michael Gibson show.

HANNAH'S TREASURE

After I came back from the mission field, I had to go to a public school called Kickapoo. I knew a couple people, but not a lot. During lunch, I would sit down and all the girls started gossiping and saying, "Oh, my gosh, that girl's so ugly. Do you know she's dating blah, blah, blah? She's so fat."

I would just sit there and think *what a mess* because I wasn't used to the shallowness and materialism.

It took me a while, but I realized that I didn't care about the same things they did. Somehow, through my life experiences, I wasn't as materialistic. But more than that, I realized I'd learned to honor God and people, more than popularity and things like clothes, purses, and boyfriends.

I ended up loving God and people more out of that experience.

MURPHY'S PEARLS

In 2010, my family started the process of adopting a little girl from China named Annie. All through the process, I was pretty excited to have a little sister.

A year and a half later, the whole family went to China to get Annie. And as soon as I got there, the excitement faded out for me, and I became really scared. My parents were so focused on her.

It was hard to lose the attention, especially because I was twelve years old. That's a time of a lot of development for a kid, and you need that attention.

I was actually bitter towards Annie for a while. Once we were home, I didn't want her to have any attention. I wanted people to focus on me. But it's definitely gotten a lot better as I've matured. I realized that she needed the attention and time more than I did.

Now she's like one of my best friends. I love the little kid so much. But yeah, that just shows how a good situation can come from bad. It was a treasure hunt . . . the mighty, mighty hunt.

MICHAEL'S TREASURE TRAVELS

In 2008, we adopted my sister—a little girl named Zoey. I wasn't really into it at first. I remember telling the social worker who came to visit us that my parents were whacked out.

And it was really hard because I couldn't understand why my parents were bringing somebody else into our family. Didn't they think my sister and I were good enough? And why were they putting all their time and energy into the adoption process?

But one of the best decisions my parents made was bringing our entire family on the journey of bringing Zoey home from Africa. It was my first time out of North America. I was surrounded by poverty and what felt like a horrible darkness. We didn't really know what we were getting ourselves into.

I remember going through a green gate to pick her up. I remember the gate opening and all the kids running toward us. I remember them bringing Zoey out, and she was so frail and none of us knew what to do.

The first time I held her in my arms, she was so sick. I stuck out my finger, and she grabbed onto it. She squeezed it as hard as she could, and I knew she was going to make it. That's when we bonded, right then and there.

In spite of the trials that I went through, thinking Mom and Dad really didn't know what they were doing, I got it right then and there.

What I really love about my family is that we make sure we operate as one unit. Nobody gets left behind. *Nobody.* We all work together.

I realized that there was more to life than just me wanting to have attention and wanting to be the center of attention. Out of this experience, I started a water well organization. Our school raised $60,000.00 to dig a well in Ethiopia. And we got to go there together as a family, where we filmed a documentary about it.

So out of the ashes of that trial experience, so many great things happened. I have an incredible sister, and I developed a passion for clean water.

Great Riches

No one tries to fall into troubles, hardships, or difficulties. Bad things simply happen to people from time to time.

I felt like my life was horrible during the mid-1970s. I was rejected, fired from my dream job, and had to move across the country to a new type of job in Texas. I was so sad, depressed, and confused as to why God would allow me to travel through such misery! But I went through it.

I hated my former boss but couldn't find any way to forgive him. I tried to forget about the pain I had suffered but found no relief. I cried out to God for two years for freedom from my painful memories. And I was mad about my poor financial conditions.

What really scared me was when I started using the exact hurtful words that my old boss had used to wound me, toward my wife and kids. I thought, *Oh, no! I'm becoming just like him!*

That really got my attention and intensified my prayers. Once I experienced the miracle of forgiveness, I started helping people who had been hurt by their mate or parents. This included teaching weekly classes for young couples who were attending Baylor University. The more I taught and counseled, the more passionate I became about the well-being of married couples and their children.

During this time in Texas I met Dr. Henry Brant. He suggested five powerful ways for me to help revive a greater number of married couples. All five ideas were brilliant—but totally impossible for me to do on my own.

I didn't have any extra money to invest in producing resources, my educational skills were at a sixth-grade level, and I had a full time job that would not allow me to take time off to pursue this new calling to help families.

I was stuck without miracles! But miracles are exactly what happened.

Within two years, all five of my new dreams had become real, and the rest is history. God was able to take a simple person like me and shower me with amazing opportunities in a very short time. I had to get ready for each miracle in a hurry to keep up with how quickly God brought each miracle to reality.

I even turned down an interview on national TV with Oprah because I didn't have the time to finish the opportunities God had already opened up for me. I thought after I had turned down Oprah that if God had opened that door once, He could do it again. And He did—three more times.

Hurt and unforgiveness tried to blind me—from my childhood into my early career. By the grace of God, I was able to forgive and see the hidden treasures He formed from those painful experiences.

I understand this isn't an easy concept to embrace. That's why I'm sharing these stories, to encourage you to face your past and hunt for the treasures.

In the next chapter we'll talk about a key that unlocks every other key.

— 7 —

WHO, WHY, AND HOW

When my grandson Michael was about ten years old, he lived about a block away from Norma and me. Through the woods and over the river to grandpa's house we go.

One day I was working in my office, and I saw him running towards our house. This wasn't an unusual occurrence, but then he started banging on the front door. When I let him in, I saw he'd been crying.

"What's wrong?" I asked.

"It's my mom," he sobbed. "Grandpa, she's driving me crazy!"

I was relieved, amused, and interested. Michael's mom happens to be my daughter, and I know she's a wonderful person and a great mom.

"Oh, I'm so sorry. Tell me what's happening. Come into my office."

"Grandpa, there are so many rules in my home. I have to

study at certain times. I have all these chores. It's driving me absolutely crazy!"

Then he burst into tears, saying "I have eight more years of this, and I don't think I can live through it."

I was laughing on the inside but said, "Oh, bless your heart. It's pretty tough living with her, I know."

"Oh, Grandpa, it's just horrible! What am I going to do?"

"Is this how you want to live? Do you want to live by letting people like your mom and your sister or schoolmates get on your nerves and complaining about it? Do you want to let people affect you like this?"

"No," he said. "I don't want to, but I don't know what to do."

"You want to do what I've been doing lately?" I asked.

"I'd love to … what are you doing? I can see you're changing, Grandpa, but I don't know what you've been doing."

I said, "I'm changing the way I think. Want to join me?"

With beautiful innocence he answered, "Yeah, Grandpa!"

"There are four verses I want you to learn. Within two weeks, I want you to have them memorized. We're going to meditate on these verses day and night."

We went outside and gathered four little stones, representing the four verses. Then he put those smooth stones in his pocket. Every time he felt them, he would meditate on one of those verses.

Building a Foundation

For an entire year, we focused our minds on those four verses, asking God to help us understand them and model them in our actions. And we had a lot of fun with our thinking-changing project.

One of the passages was Romans 5:3–5, which basically

says when you go through a difficult time, you can rejoice—you'll get patience, character, hope, and more of God's love.

> "Not only so, but we also glory in our sufferings, because we know that suffering produces perseverance; perseverance, character; and character, hope. And hope does not put us to shame, because God's love has been poured out into our hearts through the Holy Spirit, who has been given to us."

Michael and I memorized those verses, but more than just memorizing, we really thought about the meaning behind the words, and we asked the Holy Spirit to help us.

Twelve months passed.

One afternoon, his mom picked him up from school. Almost home, Michael called out, "Mom! I hate to say this, but I left my spelling list in my desk, and I have a test tomorrow. Can you take me back to school?"

This was the final straw for his mom. "No! I'm not taking you back because you're such an irresponsible student. You're not serious about school. I want you to feel the pain of an F tomorrow so you can remember not to do this anymore!"

He started to defend himself, but stopped. One of the verses we'd been meditating on came to his mind, and he realized he couldn't get defensive or angry at his mom. This situation was a trial, a test of his character, and he needed to rejoice.

"Mom, can I say something?"

Silence.

"Mom, I just want to thank you for what you're saying to me right now. You're so right-on. I'm a terrible student. And I realize that, and I thank you for reminding me. It's exactly true, Mom."

More silence from Kari as Michael continued.

"And I want you to know, Mom, you're the best mom a son could have. You're just amazing—all you do for me, how you take me all these places, and so much other stuff. I just thank God for you because God is using you in my life, right now even, to remind me of really important things."

Kari later told me, "I was so stunned. I didn't know what to say. I started crying. I literally had to pull over and take it all in before we turned the car around to take him back to school. I was wondering where in the world this change had come from."

It came from him praying about those four passages of Scripture and meditating on them for a year.

Never Too Late

Thankfully, by the time my grandchildren were around, I'd begun to go deeper into the truth of God's Word and apply His promises to family life.

It all started with a simple question.

I was in my late-fifties when a friend shook my world with a pop quiz. The question changed the entire direction of my life!

Steven K. Scott[4] asked me, "How many of Jesus' teachings can you remember right now?"

I was a bit embarrassed to realize that I hadn't really meditated on His truths, stories, and promises in a way that made them relevant to my everyday life, my marriage, kids, and grandkids.

Since that time I've memorized, or have become very familiar with, over one hundred of Jesus' teachings. But why?

Our Foundation for Family

Jesus said in John 15:5, "I am the vine; you are the branches. If you remain in me and I in you, you will bear much fruit; apart from me you can do nothing."

Just imagine people hearing those words for the first time 2,000 years ago. The Creator of the universe, the Word made flesh and blood, and the Creator of family, speaking directly to us.

Jesus even told us His words are important.

> "Why are you so polite with me, always saying 'Yes, sir,' and 'That's right, sir,' but never doing a thing I tell you? These *words* I speak to you are not mere additions to your life, homeowner improvements to your standard of living. They are *foundation words, words* to build a life on. If you work the words into your life, you are like a smart carpenter who dug deep and laid the foundation of his house on bedrock. When the river burst its banks and crashed against the house, nothing could shake it; it was built to last." (Luke 6:46–48, *The Message*, emphasis added)

Why is honor so important to us? Why is high value so important to our family relationships? Why is forgiveness the answer to anger? Why would we be crazy enough to look for "pearls" in the midst of pain?

The keys we're presenting here aren't just clever concepts someone thought up. Honor, forgiveness, and every other key in this book is based on our human design—how we were created to live.

The yearning for healing, forgiveness, and peace comes from deep in our hearts. The enjoyment of family is a gift from God!

These hopes are deeper than mere thoughts. Our Creator wants us to experience love, joy, and peace in our everyday lives and our everyday relationships—including our relationship with Him.

The words of Jesus both confirm our desire for a blessed life and challenge us to honor Him as we honor our families.

LET'S KEEP IN MIND THAT FAMILY IS GOD'S INVENTION, AND HE ONLY WANTS GOOD THINGS FOR HIS CHILDREN.

Words Build Relationships

Part of your generational legacy is faith. Let's keep in mind that family is God's invention, and He only wants good things for His children. In one of the oldest books in the Bible, we see clear connection between the Word of God and family.

> Love the Lord your God with all your heart and with all your soul and with all your strength. These commandments that I give you today are to be on your hearts. Impress them on your children. Talk about them when you sit at home and when you walk along the road, when you lie down and when you get up. (Deuteronomy 6:5–7)

See the progression? Love God, learn His Word, teach your children, and make His Word a part of your daily lives!

We're well aware that our words have the power to build a relationship, or tear a family apart—to honor a person, or hurt them. Through the years, I've had the privilege of learning so much from the wise words of others, and I hope my words are helpful to you.

I've been reading the words of Jesus since I was a child. But I was a grandfather when I finally saw the power of His words—not only as a model for our attitudes and actions, but as having a unique power to transform us from the inside out.

There are many gifted authors, speakers, and counselors with wise and helpful information. But only the words of Jesus can bring true change and healing through the power of the Holy Spirit.

Jesus made the connection clear for us in John 14:15–17:

> "If you love me, keep my commands. And I will ask the Father, and he will give you another advocate to help you and be with you forever—the Spirit of truth. The world cannot accept him, because it neither sees him nor knows him. But you know him, for he lives with you and will be in you."

Then He continues in verses 25–26:

> "All this I have spoken while still with you. But the Advocate, the Holy Spirit, whom the Father will send in my name, will teach you all things and will remind you of everything I have said to you."

Time to Engage

Perhaps you consider yourself a believer but haven't engaged with the promises found in the New Testament. You might still wonder if they're relevant to your relationships. I lived for years without really grasping the transformational force behind the Words of Jesus.

Let's be honest, many times we avoid reading the Bible because we have wrong expectations. We believe the words will only bring condemnation and guilt. I understand. Many times, scripture verses have been used to divide and condemn people. Maybe you've experienced this firsthand.

Take a fresh look at what Jesus said in John 3:16: "For God so loved the world that he gave his one and only Son, that whoever believes in him shall not perish but have eternal life."

Does this sound like God is against you, or for you?

Of course, for many of us, this verse is so common we miss the real impact. In particular, the love God has for us, and the value He places on us, and the miracle of forgiveness He wants to shower upon us. But there's more. In the next breath, Jesus said these words: "For God did not send his Son into the world to condemn the world, but to save the world through him" (John 3:17).

Read those words again, and let the truth of God's love recalibrate your thinking and give you hope. Your desire for healthy, loving, and joyful relationships comes directly from God's desire for you to experience those blessings in your life.

God has unimaginable honor and love for you. You can trust His words for your life and for your family. You can introduce the words of Jesus to your family. Through the Holy Spirit, you'll grow together in love and honor.

I will learn, understand, and model the teachings of Jesus—His words—knowing I can't live them without God's help.

Yes, some of Jesus' teachings are promises to us, like "If you remain in me and my words remain in you, ask whatever you wish, and it will be done for you" (John 15:7). In the history of mankind, who has ever said something so astounding and so full of promise?

Of course Jesus offers challenge, but can you see what He's showing us? God wants goodness for our lives and our families. He wants our lives to be solid and unshakable! We don't have to be perfect. We simply need to believe, like a child. How amazing and wonderful!

> " YOUR DESIRE FOR HEALTHY, LOVING, AND JOYFUL RELATIONSHIPS COMES DIRECTLY FROM GOD'S DESIRE FOR YOU TO EXPERIENCE THOSE BLESSINGS IN YOUR LIFE.

I've found God's promises to be true for me. My kids have found them true, and so have my grandkids. One hundred years from now? Still true—words to build a life upon and words to build generations of love and honor.

Inside Out

If you want to see changes in your spouse or kids, don't try to change them. If you want to see changes in yourself, don't rely on your own efforts.

I've tried both, and the only result was anger (and frustration). Instead, change your own attitudes from the inside out. Consider the teachings of Jesus in the everyday happenings of life. Apply them in the messiness of your relationships. Invite your spouse, your kids, and your grandkids to join you.

But don't put your trust in your own will—the Holy Spirit will do the work of transformation and growth within you.

Brain Change

When you engage your heart, soul, and mind on the words of Jesus, your life will change. In fact, the neuroscientist who helped me understand this concept is Dr. Caroline Leaf. Here's what she taught me about really valuing the words of Jesus.

Every thought we have actually develops chemically and electrically. This process takes at least thirty seconds, and the lasting impact depends on how emotionally involved we are. The more emotion we put into a thought, the bigger the change in our brains.[5]

Here's a practical example: Jesus said in Matthew 5:3, "Blessed are the poor in spirit, for theirs is the kingdom of heaven." At first those words might not make sense. But if we focus our attention, and ask God for help, all kinds of practical insight will emerge.

If I remain needy in spirit, I'm going to experience more of God's kingdom. The kingdom of God is righteousness, peace, and joy in the Holy Spirit (see Romans 14:17). The more I admit my need and seek my answers from God, the more He will provide! Yes, this is quite humbling, but then I remember God only gives His grace to the humble. God resists the proud, who say, "I can control this habit! I can change myself."

I love remaining in the attitude of a helpless beggar, because God only gives His grace and power to change to those who admit their need. We must get past our prideful inhibitions and say "Please God, I cry out to you. Out of your unlimited resources in heaven, give me strength with power through your Holy Spirit living within me."

There's such a night and day difference between reading

and meditating on the teachings of Jesus. For example, if I honor my wife, I honor her words. I'll keep her words in mind throughout my day and in the choices I make. (Especially when deciding what to order for lunch—I can almost hear her voice!) And I'll not only listen to her, I'll consider what's really behind her words. What do her words reveal about her heart and feelings?

We can meditate on Scripture the same way.

Believe

Can you see the impact that Jesus' promises can have on your thoughts and actions? Imagine the growth and transformation happening as you and your family receive a deep, heartfelt revelation of how much God values and loves them! Your kids need to be rooted and grounded in the love of Christ. As they memorize the teachings of Jesus, they begin to grasp this life-changing truth. I've seen the effects in my kids, grandkids, and finally—in myself!

But let's be clear, this is not "behavior modification." Memorizing, pondering, and praying the teachings of Jesus is cooperating with our Creator and connecting with His power to change us. His words can change us from the inside out! His words are worthy of honor.

I was sixty five years old when I realized that I'd read the teachings of Jesus but couldn't speak any of them from my heart— because His words weren't abiding in me. I hadn't committed any of them to memory.

So the first step I took was to select four passages and grab onto them with everything in me. Over and over I went through these steps:

1. Read the words slowly and carefully, to understand each word.
2. Feel the emotion behind the words.
3. Ask the Holy Spirit what He wants me to see and hear in them.
4. Read my favorite commentators on each of the verses.

Then I rinse and repeat. Yes, I rinse my human thoughts out of my head and admit that I need to think like God does. Then I repeat the process. I figure if it works for shampoo in my hair, it works for cleaning my thinking, too!

Here are four passages to start with:

1. **Matthew 5:3.** "Blessed are the poor in spirit, for theirs is the kingdom of heaven."
2. **Mark 12:30–31.** "'Love the Lord your God with all your heart and with all your soul and with all your mind and with all your strength.' The second is this: 'Love your neighbor as yourself.' There is no commandment greater than these."
3. **John 15:9–12.** "As the Father has loved me, so have I loved you. Now remain in my love. If you keep my commands, you will remain in my love, just as I have kept my Father's commands and remain in his love. I have told you this so that my joy may be in you and that your joy may be complete. My command is this: Love each other as I have loved you."

4. **Matthew 5:10–12.** "Blessed are those who are persecuted because of righteousness, for theirs is the kingdom of heaven. Blessed are you when people insult you, persecute you and falsely say all kinds of evil against you because of me. Rejoice and be glad, because great is your reward in heaven, for in the same way they persecuted the prophets who were before you."

Ripples

I hope you see how this chapter fits into a book about creating generations of loving families. Positive change in our world begins with positive change in a family. And families change when men and women humble themselves and connect with a loving God.

Why go it alone?

If, after decades of helping couples and parents, I had a more effective way to guide you to health, I would present the path right here. Look around in your world. Are the alternatives working? The best way to change your family is to change your thinking. As your thinking is elevated by the words of Jesus, you'll be able to model those words in your actions.

We all know actions speak louder than words. We've all promised to change and failed. There's a better way. Begin by humbling yourself, like a child.

God gives grace to the humble.

8

FIVE M'S FOR YOUR FAMILY

The big turning point in my life came when I lost it all.
I lost all my past anger through God's gift—the miracle of
forgiveness. This was an ending and a beginning. Suddenly my
eyes were open to the possibilities God had for my life, for my
family, and for other families.

The more anger that you hold within your heart, the deeper
the darkness in your path (see 1 John 2:9–11). If you remain in
darkness for any length of time, everything good fades from your
soul. As it says in Proverbs 4:23, "Above all else, guard your heart,
for everything you do flows from it."

I began to think and pray, "Okay, Lord. Since You were so
faithful about answering my prayer and giving me the miracle of
forgiveness, what do you want me to do with my life?"

The topics of marriage and family kept coming up and
pulling on my heart strings. My job at the church in Waco did

involve ministering to married couples, although up to this point this area wasn't something I was passionate about. Now, everywhere I looked, I saw how much help people needed in their marriages. My heart was captivated, and breaking, for the needs of families—not just in our church but around the world!

A Dream for My Life

One day a church board member and I drove around town together. I'd only been on staff at the church for twenty-four months, and he wanted to get to know me better. At one point, after a long silence, he asked me, "What are you dreaming about doing in life?"

I hesitated. After all, I was fairly new to the church and didn't want to give the impression I wasn't grateful for my job. "Well, my dream is to somehow serve marriages and families around the world, so it's a big dream . . . bigger than Waco, Texas, and I can't get the vision out of my mind!"

And he said to me, "That's pretty exciting because God's been laying it on my heart to financially support someone who's going to be in a ministry, affecting families and marriages worldwide."

I was so relieved, excited, and then terrified. *What if he tells the pastor and the rest of the church board? I'll lose my job!* But there was no need to worry.

Shortly after our conversation, a couple unexpectedly arrived at my house and rang the doorbell. "We're really kind of embarrassed to just show up without calling. You don't know us very well, but we feel God has put on our hearts to say you're going to take the broken-down walls of marriages, and you're going to help couples rebuild, with the power of God."

If this wasn't amazing and unsettling enough, within a month, two other couples arrived at our home with the very same message. All three referenced the book of Isaiah, chapter 61, and how God could use me to help rebuild the broken-down walls of marriages and families.

I began to share this vision with certain people, not sure exactly how God was leading me but amazed by the doors that were opening. However, not all open doors seemed like a blessing at the time.

The leaders of my church asked me, "We need a college Sunday school class. Would you teach it?" I didn't want to. My focus was on marriage and family, not college kids.

But guess what? Those classes were instrumental in reaching more people. To my surprise, the Sunday school gathering grew in attendance to about four hundred. We started teaching about a husband's responsibility towards his wife; and what a wife's responsibility is towards her husband.

During our first year, I developed eight different guidelines for husbands and eight guidelines for wives. By the following year, our eight teachings became ten. For four years, these college kids grew up hearing this over and over again. But I expanded the messages every year, adding more good stories and bad jokes.

The whole experience forced me to learn more about the ministry I was called into, and made me a better communicator.

Asking, Seeking, Knocking

While my calling seemed clear, my continual prayer was, "Lord, how do you want me to help families?"

Have you ever had an idea that wouldn't go away? One that kept popping into your mind? Well, I had an idea to meet with

> WHEN GOD GIVES YOU THE DESIRE FOR WHAT HE WANTS YOU TO DO, NOTHING IS IMPOSSIBLE.

Dr. Henry Brandt, a world famous psychologist. I was a bit nervous about contacting him but felt like God was answering my prayer with this internal nudge of guidance.

In our meeting I asked him, "What do you think I should do to help people in their relationships?"

"That's easy," He answered. "I've spent sixty years helping couples. You've got to do five things."

I was astounded how quickly he fired off the list, "First, you've got to write a book about what you're learning in your own marriage and family."

Write a book? I laughed inside because, as you now know, academically I'm on a sixth-grade level. And I still type about thirty words a minute with ten mistakes per line!

But here's what's really amazing about this story. When God gives you the desire for what He wants you to do, nothing is impossible. When God helped me learn to forgive, my faith was elevated to a simple childlike level. Despite the fact that we were barely surviving financially, and despite my lack of education, somehow I just knew God was going to take care of my family, and my calling.

Every day, I simply asked God to help me do what I could not do. Within two years, all five of those impossible steps became a reality. Every one of them—way beyond my wildest imagination.

Remember the college Sunday school class I didn't want to teach? Well, when those students went back home, they told their pastors about how much they enjoyed the marriage classes. This led to church invitations from all across the country! The Sunday school opportunity seemed like an ugly oyster at the time, but God had so many pearls in store for me.

This is the story of my life—miracles of forgiveness and grace, with a childlike faith always reaching out for more.

Now I want to share our sixth key: five practical principles that I call the five M's.

---

⑥

I agree to live by the five M's: (1) honor my Master, (2) honor His mission for me, (3) understand my methods in this mission, (4) learn what works to move forward, and (5) value my mate (present or future mate).

These are important for your own journey, as conversations to help align your marriage, and as a path to guide your kids. The love of God is our primary source of strength and hope. But we must make our own wise choices if we hope for a better life and a healthier family.

Here's the first and most important of the five M's.

1. Master

We all follow someone. It might be a spouse, your own whim, a parent, or someone's philosophy. You're either the boss of your life or someone else is.

Whenever I lived life as one under the authority of the

Master, God's guidance and blessing were always evident. When I chose to operate as CEO of my own little world, I often made poor choices, which hurt me, my family, and others.

If we decide to establish Christ and His words as Master of our lives, what He says is what we do. It's decided. Amazingly, Jesus modeled this very principle Himself, telling His disciples that He only did the will of His Father. He was absolutely obedient to His Father in heaven. What an amazing example, from a wonderful Master!

Think about the writers, philosophers, or heroes who are major influencers—those who affect your thinking and decisions. Are they worthy of being called your master? Some choose to bow to their emotions, selfishness, or addictions. These masters will destroy you. Jesus wants to restore you.

Our Master, Jesus, has two top commands: love God, and love others (Matthew 22:37–39). Those are remarkable, and for me, prove Him as a trustworthy, kind master. When I read this, my heart cries out to learn from, and trust in, this one true Master. Not only does Jesus ask us to love, He gives us the ability to love and the power to forgive.

Not only does He command us to honor our families, He first honors us with His love, so we're able to value and care for them. Because of this, our first response and responsibility is to humble ourselves and believe His ways are the best for us.

Have you ever humbled yourself and cried out to Jesus as your Master? A follower of Christ is simply a person who believes that what He says is from God. All I do is jump off of my life map and I jump onto God's life map.

I must tell you, none of these keys really work without this genuine relationship with Christ. So if you're reading this and realizing you don't have one, here's your opportunity. Our family invites you to step away from your own life map and step onto His. You can do this right now, before you finish this book.

> TRUST IN THE LORD WITH ALL YOUR HEART. DON'T TRY TO FIGURE THIS OUT ON YOUR OWN.

Maybe you have been a follower of the Good Master, but you're feeling challenged by the Holy Spirit. You might have some idols. I understand the temptation to trust in your job, your money, your parents, or your spouse instead of Him. Make Jesus Christ your Master.

Trust in the Lord with all your heart. Don't try to figure this out on your own. In all your ways submit to Him and He will make your paths straight (Proverbs 3:6). That's what I've done with my family, and that's the reason you're reading this book!

Simply say this to God:

Master, Jesus, I trust You with all my heart. I trust in your Words. I trust You with my life and my forever. I need you, because I believe You are who You said You were. I believe You rose from the dead. I believe You. So right now, I give you my life. I ask you to teach me how to live.

Now we're all part of the same family—God's family! And we have a wonderful Father, Counselor, and Master. You don't have to do family all by yourself—do family together with God's help!

2. Mission

Good news: If you've decided to follow the Master, you have a *mission*. The question is, what mission does Jesus have for you?

As a young man, I didn't want to forgive the man who betrayed me, but my Master commanded me to forgive. By the grace of God, I finally obeyed His loving command, released the anger, and the mission of my life was unlocked.

The first step to knowing your mission is pretty simple. Since Jesus is my Master, I simply ask Him to show me clearly what His mission is for me! (And I ask, and ask, and ask!) I try to understand how God made me so I can best serve Him. Once I have peace inside of me about the mission He has for me, I start getting ready to do it. That's our part.

We know His mission is for us to love people, but more specifically, you can ask yourself what you have a strong desire to do for others. For example, do you want to help relieve people of physical pain? Then there are hundreds of ways you can step into helping people. You might begin as a volunteer, or take a class, or meet with a professional in your area of interest.

Do you love entertaining people and making them laugh? Do you feel called to talk to people about God's love and salvation? Do you feel passionate about teaching others? As I hope you've seen in my story, your heart's desires are not random coincidences or whims. The love-powered ideas rise from your heart and point toward your mission!

Keep asking God to show you steps to take in your mission! He might even direct people to show up at your door with a confirming word!

Can you see how important a sense of mission is for you—and for your children! Look at high-school and college students today. Because so many lack a clear mission, their lives are rudderless.

In the context of this book, I know a lot about your mission. We all share a calling to honor God as Master. We're all called to honor our family members as we honor ourselves. Your every-single-day mission is to release anger and give forgiveness. And we all have the mission of treasure hunting—digging for the good in the bad.

In all these missions, you also have the honor of helping your family members to honor, forgive, and treasure hunt. Start there, and trust God to show you more about the other areas of your life and your family members' lives.

How do you have mission-conversations with your spouse, to help each other discover your mission? Here are some insights from my son, Michael, and his wife, Amy.

MISSION IN MARRIAGE

Dream together. And notice together. Be intentional with each other, noticing who your mate is and what they might be passionate about. Then encourage those areas.

I can't imagine Amy not being a part of our ministry to couples, but early in our marriage, she was hesitant. I knew she was struggling, but I simply pointed out the potential I saw in her in an encouraging way.

"I see your passion for the Lord and a passion for the couples I'm working with. So it makes sense that you might want to be involved." This process of encouragement took place over several years, not thirty days. It was a constant encouragement. "Amy, I can see you doing this. I believe you can."

As you take steps together in your mission, enjoy the learning process! Here's my wife, Amy's perspective:

Michael continued to encourage me. He asked good questions, and he allowed me to fail. As a young girl, I was a gymnast, but I wasn't very good because I was terrified of landing on my head. The fear was more compelling than the desire to accomplish the goal. I didn't have the confidence to try or the confidence to succeed.

That's something Michael has instilled in me and our kids. Any time they fell, he would say, "Oh, my gosh, that's so awesome. You did a great job! You tried that! You did your best."

I never had that kind of encouragement as a child, so I was scared of failing, even as an adult. I would wonder *What if I embarrass myself?* And Michael would say, "So what?" He gave me room to fail, which gave me room to succeed!

In my first marriage-intensive I was talking with a couple, let's call them Betty and Bob. Well, Betty had an affair with someone named Fred. Despite my best efforts, I kept calling the husband Fred. Yes, really.

It was a disaster—not for the couple but for me. But Michael calmly said, "Amy, aren't you glad you got that one out of your system?"

And I was like, "No! That was the most horrifying, embarrassing experience in the world!"

The next day, the couple stunned me . . . by coming back! We had a wonderful session!

Today, as I train coaches in how to do marriage-intensives, this story is a highlight. I tell people, "Your intensive can't go any worse than my first intensive!" I suppose that's treasure hunting . . . right?

NURTURING MISSION

Ask your kids what they're passionate about. Pay attention to activities your children are interested in. Notice what makes them excited about getting up in the morning. Ask them questions and explore these areas with them. These conversations create a sense of safety. When your children feel safe to express their interests and dreams, their mission will begin to emerge.

> **WHEN YOUR CHILDREN FEEL SAFE TO EXPRESS THEIR INTERESTS AND DREAMS, THEIR MISSION WILL BEGIN TO EMERGE.**

Grandparent, aunts, and uncles play an important role in helping kids discover their mission.

For all three of my children, and now with my grandchildren, I pictured a special future for each . . . but only after studying them for a long time.

Kari was a natural teacher and storyteller. Greg was such a great negotiator and seemed like he'd make a good lawyer. Michael was a super speaker and comedian.

Norma and I always reminded them that we would support them in whatever areas of life they chose. But we also knew that to truly love and honor our kids, we needed to recognize and nurture their God-given interests.

3. Methods

The third M is for *methods*. Once you have a strong sense of your mission, the methods and action steps become important. Remember, right now we all have the clear mission of loving our family as we would want to be loved. That's a pretty big mission in itself.

In the process, we also have the honor of exploring and choosing possible methods to live our mission. Your family needs to see this method-finding in action! For example, if your mission involves being a veterinarian, you'll apply to the best schools and try to obtain the best training and experience.

The five key pieces of advice Dr. Brandt gave me were methods! They were: write books, create ten messages for couples, use videos, speak at conferences, and counsel couples privately. At first, each seemed impossible, but I took baby-steps toward each one.

Ask, and keep asking God for wisdom and direction to guide you along the path!

> **I SIMPLY KEEP FAILING FORWARD IN MY QUEST TO BE A BLESSING TO MY FAMILY AND THOSE GOD PUTS IN MY PATH.**

WHAT IF I FAIL?

Fear of failure leads directly to failure.

Even if you've failed many times, you're one step closer to succeeding. God still wants to use you. His mission for you never changes and is never revoked.

Hopefully you're getting a picture of what this looks like from my life and my efforts to build a healthy family. I simply keep failing forward in my quest to be a blessing to my family and those God puts in my path.

METHODS FOR BLESSING YOUR CHILDREN

The five blessing actions that John Trent and I wrote about in our book, *The Blessing*, are examples of methods.

The first action is "meaningful touch." Parents can use hugs, holding hands, or an arm around a shoulder to check the condition of their child's heart. If the child is angry, you'll have an opportunity to help them release their anger. And we can always use touch as a way to show value and affection.

The second method is "spoken message." Verbally expressing to your kids, "I love you, and nothing will ever stop me from loving you," is an example of the power of your words to bless your child.

In some Jewish homes, there's a tradition of a weekly blessing. On Friday nights, the father walks around his family, placing his hand on each of their heads as he speaks blessings to them. This practice combines touch and message, and also shows he highly values them, which is the third method of blessing.

"Attaching high value" to your children means you see their value, as in our story of the yellow diamonds, and you show their value by your actions.

The fourth blessing action is affirming a special future for your children. I would always try to say to my kids regularly, "Gosh, you'd be so great in this area!" And they were all positively influenced by those observations.

The fifth method is "lasting commitment." In other words, expressing with words and actions, "I will love you forever, no matter what you do."

These five methods will help build a framework for your family and for generations to come.

4. Move Forward

The fourth M is *move forward*. More specifically, maintain the good methods that are working for you and your family. Sometimes it's easier to make a change than it is to actually maintain the change.

Lasting growth happens in you and your family when you keep moving forward, using methods that work. Your core mission doesn't change, but you might need to use more effective methods along the way.

When your family has a sense of mission, conversations and action steps about methods will bring you closer together. Moving forward also applies to our prayer life. There is power in determined prayer.

One of Jesus' parable teachings on the subject describes an elderly widow who was so determined to get what she needed that she kept asking, and asking, and asking! Jesus used this illustration to remind us to never give up in our prayers (Luke 18).

This is actually my posture in prayer. Like a helpless old lady, I ask, seek, and knock for direction, answers, and provision, continually humbling myself before the Master and trusting like a child that He will help.

As you set out to honor your spouse, you may experience discouraging setbacks and explosions of anger. Keep praying, keep honoring, and release your anger along the way.

"But Gary, I've been trying to honor my wife for a week, and our arguments are getting worse!"

Keep moving forward. Building a healthy marriage and family takes time. So many couples make a decision to forgive, or treasure hunt, but when their relationship isn't transformed overnight, they quit. Wonderful blessings await those who, with God's help, keep moving forward.

HELP YOUR KIDS MOVE FORWARD

God has a mission for your kids. It's your responsibility to help them discover wise methods to pursue their calling.

When our kids were young, Norma and I praised everything and anything that they loved doing. We also looked for areas where they seemed naturally gifted. This affirmation is vital for your children.

The point of parenting is not to control your child. The goal is to release them where they seemed naturally gifted. This affirmation is a vital force in the shaping of society.

Our son Michael couldn't wait to leave home when he turned eighteen, not because of anger but because he was ready. He was ready, so we didn't need to lay any of our expectations on him. He was on the right track, and we were there to cheer him on!

Imagine generations of children learning to humbly discover their mission and moving forward to grow into their calling!

5. Your Mate

The fifth M is for your *mate.*

Healthy families begin with a healthy marriage. The principles we're presenting in this book can be applied to building a loving, joyful marriage, which is your most important relationship.

You've got to do whatever you can to have a thriving marriage, because if that relationship's not working, all your other relationships will suffer.

No human bond matches the intensity, and the importance, of marriage in terms of your life and legacy. If your marriage is troubled, your parenting will be affected negatively.

Practically speaking, if you're stressed out, your career will suffer, and you'll be more likely to have health problems. These issues will only put more strain on your marriage, and the effect snowballs!

Marriage is the foundation for family. That's why it's so important to invest in it. That's why you can *make* time, because there's nothing more important. You might think you need to do another hour at work, but you don't—because that's an hour less for your marriage.

Many who continue in misplaced priorities of job and marriage will lose both!

SINGLE

If you're single, choose a mate who is moving in the same direction as you are—with the same Master and mission.

Talk about Master, mission, and methods with a potential spouse. Pay attention—are they *"Moving Forward?"* If you want harmony in your marriage, don't settle for a mate who isn't aligned with you and your mission.

Many couples are choosing not to get married these days. Why? For many, it's because their parents were not getting along; they weren't honoring each other. They were divorcing at an astonishing rate.

NO HUMAN BOND MATCHES THE INTENSITY, AND THE IMPORTANCE, OF MARRIAGE IN TERMS OF YOUR LIFE AND LEGACY.

Children grow up with that and conclude, "I don't want marriage. There's nothing but pain and suffering." Some, maybe you, blame themselves, and carry anger and unforgiveness toward themselves. *If I'd been a better son or daughter . . . if I'd been an easier kid . . . if I'd been more successful . . . then my mom and dad wouldn't have divorced.*

Again, my family isn't perfect, but I'm thankful to say we love and enjoy each other. We have a family worth repeating. You can, too.

FUTURE MATES OF YOUR CHILDREN

Talk to your kids about marriage, and about their future mates.

Here's one of the ways I've done this with my sons.

"Someday when you want to date a young lady, how would

that look?"

"What do you mean?"

"Well, for example, how are you going to treat her someday when you ask someone out? How are you going to behave around her?"

That's when you coach them, or hear them say, "I'll treat her as highly valuable. I'll be considerate, and open the door for her."

"I want you to imagine that you're a marrying age. You've met someone special. What's she like? What does she do? What kind of character does she have?"

Many people go into relationships ignorant and blind. They don't even think about the qualities they value. Because of this, they're susceptible to the moment and the lure of physical pleasure.

It's very reactionary. That's why taking time to consider and write down character traits is so helpful.

Here's an example of what a "Qualities of a Future Mate" list can look like for a girl:

- Treats me like a queen
- He's a Christian
- Has a great personality (funny, sweet, and a gentleman)
- Enjoys sports
- Loves his family and loves my family
- Makes me feel safe
- Is kind to all
- Can bond with my dad and brother
- Doesn't cuss
- Has the approval of my family
- Doesn't try to change me or blame me

Here's some more on this point from my son-in-law, Roger Gibson.

A VISION

My wife, Kari, and I have initiated similar talks with our kids, engaging them in conversations about what their future mate might "look" like—not from a physical standpoint, but personality traits, hobbies, and spirituality.

It's really special to go through these lists with your kids because you can also start helping them direct what they look for in a mate. What are the traits of a Christ-centered man? What are the characteristics of a godly woman?

We're talking about another spiritual conversation to have with your kids. For example, when your daughter meets a young man, you can ask her, "How does this fella rank with the twenty traits you wrote down?" So this isn't the first talk, or prayer, you've had on the subject of a future mate.

This keeps your kids on the path of intentionality and helps them process emotions. As a parent, instead of being a bad cop, you're a guide, reminding your child of what they really want in a mate.

The M and M's

Norma and I have seen the 5 M's played out in our kids' lives, our grandkids' lives, and even between family units!

A few years ago, our daughter, Kari, invited her niece Taylor on a mission trip to Ethiopia and Uganda. (Taylor is Greg and Erin's daughter and our granddaughter.)

Taylor was in pre-med studies at the time, studying to become a doctor. So Kari arranged for Taylor to shadow a doctor there and do the medical rounds together. The experience ignited something in her.

Taylor, her parents, Kari, and Michael had a lot of great conversations about mission and methods in this situation. As a result, Taylor actually changed some of her university studies to align with her mission.

The five M's are ongoing—not a one-time talk or a week-long study.

- Your Master
- Your mission
- Your methods
- Moving forward
- Your mate

Establishing these topics in your family conversations will help move you towards healthy relationships and fruitful lives—even in the midst of storms.

—— 9 ——

THE RIGHT TIME

L ife has taught me this profound truth: In order to become close friends with someone, you must actually engage in some type of activity with them.

Okay, this might not be groundbreaking research. After all, some struggling families are around each other a lot, and a growing number of couples even work together. Time alone does not equal harmony.

You don't just need time together; you need the *right* time together. And I believe you're ready to try some new experiences. If you want to become close friends with your spouse, children, and grandchildren, you must spend time with each one.

Routine Disruption

Your typical daily and weekly schedules should have intentional time set aside for meals together and other family activities. These consistent experiences are crucial for a sense of safe expression, and they demonstrate value for each other.

But routines can be so . . . routine.

When your aim is to improve the quality of your marriage, or deepen the connection with your children, intentional schedule disruption is essential. Yes, trying new experiences can be scary, especially if you feel like your relationships are a bit fragile. That's why we first explored these six keys—to open hearts for healthy growth.

1. I will learn to highly honor and love each family member.

2. I will learn to keep my anger to the lowest level each day toward every family member or in any situation.

3. I will learn every way possible to forgive my family members each day or seek forgiveness when I offend any one of them. I promise to help each family member remain in family harmony as much as I'm able.

4. I will take personal responsibility to find the pearls and God's blessings from each and every trial I face.

5. I will learn and understand the words of Christ and seek God's power to daily live His words.

6. I agree to live by the five M's: honor my Master, honor His mission for me and my methods in this mission, learn what works to move me forward, and value my mate (present or future mate).

Of course, you'll want some practice with these principles. And remember to bring these keys along on your family adventures! You'll need them all.

Storm Warning

I love storms . . . especially a month after they've passed!

If you've ever lived in the Midwest, you know how those thunderstorms can explode out of nowhere. One night, a violent storm erupted. Greg and Kari were just three and five at the time, and Michael wasn't yet born. Norma and I huddled close in bed, wondering what to do. *Should we wake the kids?* I tried to calculate the distance of the lightning strikes, based on the time between the flash and the boom. *Is it one second per mile away? Five seconds per mile?*

A bright flash exploded with a deafening clap that seemed to come from directly above. Our roof actually started flapping from the violent gusts topping fifty miles an hour, as rainwater started to drip on us. We were terrified. We were camping together, in a borrowed pop-up camper. Norma and I held hands and shivered together, neither saying a word.

"Do you think the trailer is going to blow over?" Norma whispered.

"Not a chance," I bravely stuttered.

I was thinking, *We're not going to blow over, we're going to blow up!* I kept noticing the metal frame, each time the lighting flashed. *We're doomed!*

The storm went on for what seemed like an hour, then finally calmed.

We survived our first night of family bonding. By the way,

Greg and Kari slept through the whole experience. Norma and I were literally "closer" during and after because we couldn't stop holding each other!

The next morning, Norma and I looked at each other and asked, "Is this really the key to a close-knit family?"

Legendary Battles

My early marriage research seemed to reveal that experiences like these were crucial to a healthy family, so we kept on camping. After one four-day excursion of sand-filled sleeping bags, we were all exhausted and looking forward to being back home (which is really a wonderful feeling when you stop to consider it). About two hundred miles from our house in Chicago, the kids were driving Norma and me crazy with the usual fighting and noise. So we stopped at a Stuckey's roadside oasis to fill the fuel tank and grab some snacks.

Some toys caught my eye, so I picked up a little doll for Kari and one of those suction-cup dart guns with a little target for Greg. *That'll keep them busy*, I thought.

It only took Greg three minutes to figure out he could remove the mini-plunger from his darts. Our newfound peace and quiet was suddenly interrupted by a "click" followed immediately by a piercing cry from Norma. The newly fashioned weapon hit the passenger-seat window at the precise angle to ricochet onto Norma's ear.

I could tell the pain was quite intense, especially since she started scrambling into the back seat to disarm Greg.

Let's be real. We'd had it with the kids.

As we settled back into our home and unpacked, we said to each other, "We'll never camp again. Never!" It was miserable and uncomfortable.

A Method That Moved Us Forward

About three weeks later, something strange happened. I noticed we were all laughing about our recent trip—even the dart gun incident. And we all seemed closer. We liked each other more.

Shortly after these rookie outdoor adventures, I started interviewing couples with children. I would even look for certain people in the audience at our seminars—families who really seemed to enjoy each other. During my talks, they would laugh together, elbow each other, and give knowing, affectionate looks to each other.

I would approach them during the break, "Can I interview you guys after the session?" In our time together, I would ask, "Why do you think you're so in love?" and "Why do you enjoy being with each other?"

Every single family replied, "Camping." I must have interviewed at least fifty families, and each one camped together, whether in tents, trailers, or motor homes. They would say, "Well, camping is just so much fun." Not one mentioned the lack of sleep, annoying insects, the arguments, or mini-arrow scars. This wasn't a scientific study, but it confirmed my suspicion about the benefits of venturing out into the unknown as a family.

> SINCE COMMUNICATION IS THE NUMBER ONE KEY OF A THRIVING MARRIAGE AND FAMILY, YOU MUST CREATE OPEN OPPORTUNITIES TO TALK.

So the Smalley family camped from then on, until all our kids were through college. And guess what? All our kids take their kids camping.

This is a *method* that worked for our family, eventually, so we made a commitment to *move forward* with our camping adventures.

Scheduled Disasters

The point is, we schedule time to be together.

Norma and I schedule lunch and walks with each other. We talk; I listen.

Since communication is the number one key of a thriving marriage and family, you must create open opportunities to talk, which leads us to our seventh key:

I will try to meet face to face with as many family members as possible to remain bonded in harmony with them.

The more time to open up for listening, the more you'll be able to understand each other. The more you understand each other, the closer you become. Yes, there's intentional effort, inconvenience, and some hard choices involved.

One of the best ways to create lasting relational bonds is to struggle together against a common crisis. This is true for any relationship and any kind of family—blended families, adoptive families, or single parent homes. Sometimes the common crisis is a hungry swarm of mosquitos, sometimes it's getting lost in unfamiliar territory, and sometimes it's burning dinner beyond recognition.

Camping is one of the best examples of a bonding experience because you're actually scheduling a disaster—maybe several. But if you pack honor, forgiveness, and a sense of humor, you'll discover priceless treasures together. Really.

No Pressure

Expect imperfect. Expect little arrows, and expect some pain.

So many couples don't plan adventures because they're afraid of imperfection. They want picture-postcard experiences where every moment is blissful. But let me share a bit of wisdom: Bliss comes in learning how to handle disaster.

You know about LUV talk. Practice it at home, in the car, and especially in the midst of chaos.

Adventures like camping will reveal all sorts of treasures—hidden treasures—although it might take a few hours, or a few weeks, for those ugly oysters to open up.

Here's a story from my son-in-law, Roger.

NATURE CALLS

Kari and I had just celebrated our son Michael's first birthday. So we went camping . . . the first time as a family. What could possibly go wrong?

We arrived at the campground, delighted to have our pick of beautiful sites by the river. We had the place to ourselves.

Everything was going beautifully. We looked like we were auditioning for a tourist brochure, or at least we felt that way. I set up camp while Kari and Michael played, enjoying the fresh air and the wide sunset.

Campers, it turns out, have bladders, too. Soon it was Kari's turn to go to the restroom, which was actually an outhouse. The sign inside didn't help: "Please don't throw sticks down there, because what's inside could pole-vault out!"

A few seconds later, she returned at a brisk pace. "There are things moving under that shack," she reported.

I laughed for about a millisecond.

"I'm not sitting in there. You've got to take me to a real bathroom."

The last possible location with a "real" bathroom was twenty-five miles away. So what did we do?

You guessed it. We piled in the car and zoomed to a gas station, twenty-five miles away. (Okay, twenty-four miles to be exact. I tracked the mileage and complained all the way.)

When we returned to our secluded oasis of peace, we had a difficult time locating our camp site, mainly due to the darkness . . . and the huge crowd of college kids who had invaded the campground and now surrounded our idyllic site.

Because of the noise, one-year-old Michael couldn't sleep. Finally, around 1:00 a.m., he dozed off. That's when the motorcycle gang arrived.

Best I could tell from all the Harley Davidson headlights, these were the *Hells Angels* kind of motorcycle group. From the moment they arrived, the college students seemed like amateur partiers.

We had all the exotic sights and sounds campers try to escape . . . and the smells. I'm pretty sure it was pot.

Kari tapped me on the shoulder and whispered, "I want you to go out there and tell them to be quiet."

So what did I do? I packed up the tent, escorted my young family into the truck, and went back home.

Camping adventure number one, completed!

Thankfully, we continued to camp, and our family adventures improved. Yes there were scrapes and bruises and arguments, but most of these moments turned into funny stories. We've even learned to enjoy outhouses . . . at least some of us have.

Looking Forward

Planning your outings is essential, but every outing creates the wonderful side-effect of anticipation. Having an upcoming family activity helps everyone focus on something positive and unifying.

As a family, we decided to camp once a month. As the trip date approached, one of the kids would usually have a wonderful excuse for not going along—especially as they grew into their teenage years.

I'd calmly say, "Well, we all agreed that we were going to go," and leave it there. Then a week before, or even two days before, they'd say, "You know what, I'd rather go camping with you guys."

I know this might sound like science fiction, but that's the power of honor in action!

We hold each other accountable. "Look, we need to have

family adventures to stay close as a family. And Mom and I love hanging out with you!"

Yes, you'll need to strengthen your resolve a bit, endure some eye-rolling, and learn to ignore some whining. The long-term benefits are worth it!

When you see brother holding sister accountable, and vice-versa, you know there are some wonderful bonds being created.

Deep inside, your kids are hoping you'll honor them by sticking to your commitments. That's what a healthy family does. That's what your kids need and want—despite their protests.

Plan Time Together

Not all bonding happens in a forest. The point is to be intentional, using your calendar and all means necessary to stay connected. Even technology can help you grow closer.

One hundred years ago we had two choices: face-to-face conversations or handwritten letters. Now, we can call, video chat, text, email, and use social media to build a sense of closeness. Twenty years from now, we'll probably have 3D images of our loved ones projected into the living room or dinner table!

So, today, we have two choices: fight technology or embrace it to stay in touch with family. Does video chat qualify as "face-to-face"? With loved ones residing all over the country, I've decided that it does qualify, especially because we can talk to and see videos of our grandkids whenever we want.

You don't have to go it alone when planning special family times. Make it a fun family exercise! As our kids got older, I would ask the family to sit down for a short meeting.

"Okay, here's what I need from you," I said, holding my paper and pen. "For the next twelve months, what would you like to see happen in your life, or happen as a family, so you can look back and say, 'Wow, what a great year!'"

> **THE POINT IS TO BE INTENTIONAL, USING YOUR CALENDAR AND ALL MEANS NECESSARY TO STAY CONNECTED.**

We would get some of the best ideas and insights into the desires of our kids' hearts from those meetings. And it was just as rewarding to see Norma beam while listening to our kids open up. She and I would also get to share our hopes and specific ideas.

Then we'd all say to each other, "We're going to help you have that experience!" And we worked together as a family to see those desires happen.

Norma and I wrote the items down, then printed out the lists. We'd sometimes tack them up on the kids' bedroom walls as a reminder. As our kids got older, these meetings sometimes veered into times of sharing visions of their future careers or even their future spouses!

There's no perfect way to have family meetings. It's an adventure, just like camping. Stuff will go wrong. You'll feel clumsy and unsure . . . but your family will love it.

Together Ideas

Here are some creative suggestions from our family to yours. Please note, we never said these were easy, but we promise they are worthwhile.

DAILY

- Have meals together. (Many studies prove significant benefits for families who regularly share meals together.)[6]
- While driving, turn off the music and ask questions.
- If you're out of town, talk to your spouse and kids by phone or video.

WEEKLY

- Take frequent date nights with your mate.
- Develop simple traditions: For example, my son Michael has had many meaningful conversations during "Jacuzzi Time."
- TV watching: Yes, you can initiate some wonderful discussions about the program.

MONTHLY

- Visit a zoo or a museum.
- Discover "favorite things" for each family member and participate in those together.

YEARLY

- Volunteer at a food bank or shelter .
- Attend marriage retreats.
- Take short-term mission trips.

Don't over-think these adventures. It's not the mechanics that matter—it's the experience.

It's Time

Don't let lifestyle choices, or your calendar, keep you from enjoying time together. Consider limiting your kids' activities to one at a time. Maybe they're involved in dance, music, and multiple sports at the same time. When will you share meals together as a family?

A child grows up learning, by example, about priorities in life. Sadly, the lessons many kids learn are "performance trumps family" or "money trumps family." You can't say there's not enough time.

You have time. Learn to say no to less important things. Make family a priority.

> **THERE'S NO PERFECT WAY TO HAVE FAMILY MEETINGS. IT'S AN ADVENTURE, JUST LIKE CAMPING.**

Love and Devotion

Have you noticed I haven't mentioned an obligation to lead family devotions? Have you been holding your breath, waiting for me to mandate a daily Bible study together? You can breathe easy. We've seen some families succeed at this, but for me, the pressure and expectations were just too much.

And in my work, I've talked with so many parents who feel guilty that they're not leading a formal devotional. Honestly, I never found it realistic. Does that surprise you? Most of the parents I've discussed this with are relieved when I tell them to put their focus in other areas.

Let's be honest, most devotions aren't very good, and everyone knows it. But if you'll focus on the seven keys we've shared every day, and every week, family discussions will naturally turn to the subject of honor, forgiveness, and treasure hunting.

When I tried a formal devotion, my kids would always find something funny about it. Everyone would start giggling—except me. I was serious. After all, God is a serious topic, right? Our kids laughed a lot during my serious prayers.

Earn the opportunity to give unplanned devotions and pay attention to what your children are interested in. If your child has taken an interest in a certain spiritual topic, encourage them with "Hey, what have you been thinking about that?"

Each family, and each child, is unique. You don't have to force-feed some formal structure to them. Get to know the environments where their heart is most open, and the ways they enjoy learning. You'll find that the most impactful spiritual conversations are spontaneous and rooted in a shared experience.

For example, watching the sun rise on the lake. My kids and I have shared wonderful "devotions" and open discussions in these moments. We've even had communion.

I like to ask questions. So I constantly told my kids, and tell my grandkids, that there are no bad questions. "You can always ask me anything. I'll love you no matter what—regardless of what you think, what you believe, or how you behave."

Spirituality grows best in an atmosphere of safety.

Do That Again

If you're a parent, you've heard your child say "Again!" on a playground after a fun slide, or after an exhausting piggyback ride. They don't want the moment to end.

When you venture out into new experiences as a family,

there's something deeper going on beneath the surface. Your spouse is seeing you in a different light. Your kids are forming impressions and opinions about you, and about the very idea of family. They're wondering if this thing called "marriage" is worth it—worth repeating in their lives. Children are always looking for evidence that family is a real, valuable treasure.

You're investing in them, so someday, they'll say to their spouse and their kids, *Let's do that again!*

—— 10 ——

LIVING THE SEVEN KEYS IN THE REAL WORLD

Driving home from Lake Waco, I finally rounded the corner to my driveway. I was excited to be back with my family and looking forward to reuniting with my Lazy Chair.

As I pulled up to the garage, there was an unexpected surprise. *Why is the edge of my roof torn off? How did that huge hole get into the side of our mini-motor-home?*

In my imagination, I instant-replayed the scene, picturing Norma driving the camper right into our house—in slow motion. *Oh, crud!*

I knew I'd see her in minutes—seconds maybe. I blurted out loud, "What should I say?"

Then a voice surprised me, "Why don't you say what you teach?"

It was my twelve-year-old son, Greg, who happened to be sitting next to me in the car. I was so upset, it took me a while to get my thoughts together. I actually had to stop and think, *What do I teach?*

Once again, the little voice chimed in, "Dad, you teach that Mom's more valuable than material things, money, and all that stuff."

"You're right! That's it!" I said, as we got out of the car.

I was still upset, but my anger was mixed with a new feeling—compassion for Norma.

Just then, she came walking around the corner of the house. She was crying.

"Look . . . what I did!"

I knew she felt horrible. So I didn't say a word and put my arms around her.

After almost a minute, I finally whispered, "Oh, I'm so sorry, Norma. I know you're upset, but I've had so many more wrecks than you'll ever even think about having. And I love you a lot more than this camper and a lot more than this roof, so don't worry about it. I'll have it fixed in a hurry."

"Thank you," she said, still in my embrace.

Then she quietly added, "By the way, I told the neighbors across the street about the accident. So . . . they're watching us, right now, to see how you respond."

There might as well have been a TV news crew there. In my mind, I replayed my reaction to the incident in slow motion. I was quite relieved that I had listened to the little voice, reminding me to honor people above things.

IF YOU'RE AWARE OF THE DESTRUCTIVE POWER OF ANGER, YOU'LL LEARN TO RECOGNIZE AND RELEASE YOUR ANGER QUICKLY.

Home Repairs

After a few more moments, Norma wiggled out of my arms, smiled, and skipped back inside. Surprisingly, I felt better about the whole situation, too. *Golly, this honor stuff really does work!*

Instead of reacting in anger, and selfishness, I quickly shifted my focus to how highly I value my wife. Yes, Greg's voice helped me snap back into this mindset, just like the Holy Spirit also gently reminds us.

In challenging situations like these, the best approach is to express how much you love and honor your spouse or child. Keep in mind that your family member usually feels worse about the situation than you do. Just hold them tenderly, if they're ready.

These keys actually work in the real world! Let's take another look at how we live them.

Our first two keys are:

- I will learn to highly honor and love each family member.
- I will learn to keep my anger at the lowest level each day toward every family member or in any situation.

If you've made a list of the qualities you value most about your spouse and children, you'll be able to focus intentionally on those points and to honor them in any situation.

If you're aware of the destructive power of anger, you'll learn to recognize and release your anger quickly.

With God's help, you'll hear a quiet voice reminding you

to choose honor. As you respond, your family's sense of safety will grow.

Here's a story from my daughter, Kari.

HONOR STUDENTS

I learned from my mom and dad about placing high value on people, and I brought this key into the classroom.

I taught elementary school in the inner-city of Phoenix, Arizona. Many of my students had wounded hearts and lacked confidence. My dad encouraged me to highly honor every child, every day, and allow God to work through me to encourage and build their self-image.

I accepted the challenge and made a conscious effort to pour love and honor into each child. I even brought my dad's "100 karat" diamond to teach them what value was all about.

Some students were aggressive, angry, afraid, and abused. It was truly an honor to show my students how valuable they were to me—even if I was the only person in their lives telling them how important they were as human beings. Did honor make a difference?

To this day, I receive Facebook messages, letters, and emails telling me how loved and accepted they felt in my classroom. Love and honor and value are gifts we give one another with no strings attached! Thanks, Mom and Dad for helping me grow as a teacher, wife, mom, and missionary!

Letting Go of the Past

Every person has past hurts, disappointment, and anger. Everyone.

I hope the time you've invested reading this book has been helpful. But please understand that more time is needed to grow ... and to heal.

In the work my kids do, helping marriages, they deal with people who've been hurt in relationships. Many of these couples come because they're trying to repair their marriage from the effects of an affair. The feelings don't disappear in two days. But a couple can get on the right track so they can heal properly over the course of time.

The same is true for those who've been divorced. Most remarry too quickly. They're not healed, so they carry the pain and unforgiveness into their next marriage, which is why second marriages have such a high divorce rate.

There is no substitute for time. Here's a story from my son, Michael.

MIDDLE OF THE ROAD

Early in my marriage to Amy, we had one of our worst fights. I was so hurt that I ran out of the house—in the middle of the night.

I've married the wrong person, I thought, as I lay down in the middle of the road and waited for a car to run over me. (That sounds pretty dramatic, but the odds were pretty slim at 3:00 a.m. on a semi-private country road.)

"God, I will *never* get over this fight."

One day passed, and the emotion cooled down a little. We went to counseling, and the pain healed a bit more. Then, a year later, something amazing happened, on the one-year anniversary of the fight.

I was driving down that road, over the spot where I laid down, and I knew it was over. The hurt was gone . . . completely.

Don't be too hard on yourself. Good seeds take time to grow, and bad weeds take time to wilt. When you do the things that are outlined here, including allowing the Holy Spirit to guide you, you and your family will heal.

Safety and LUV

When your family feels safe, they'll listen to each other. Together, you'll be able to talk about world events, school, work, and their relationships at home. And you'll be able to talk about anger.

Remember, when you detect anger in a family member: listen, understand, and validate them. This is LUV talk!

LISTEN

Don't react, don't interrupt, just listen. Try to hear what the other person is really saying. There are always important thoughts and feelings behind anger. Your only job is to listen.

UNDERSTAND

Understanding and agreeing are two different things. It's possible to understand but not agree. The goal here is to give the other person the honor of being understood.

VALIDATE

Value the other person, and what they feel. Let them experience some release to their anger.

> **WHEN YOUR FAMILY FEELS SAFE, THEY'LL LISTEN TO EACH OTHER.**

The next time someone in your family is upset, practice LUV talk. I think you'll both enjoy the process . . . and the results.

Here's a story from my son Greg.

YOUR KIDS ARE LISTENING

My son, Garrison, grew up hearing about how important it is for a man to honor a woman. It's funny how this showed up one time when he was having a conversation with a single friend of ours named Lindsey when he was just five years old.

She was talking about going on a date with a guy, who she is now married to. Here was their conversation:

Garrison: What movie are you going to see?

Lindsey: A movie about superheroes.

Garrison: Why are you going to that movie?

Lindsey: Because I'm going with a boy, and he picked it.

Garrison: Geoff?

Lindsey: Yes.

Garrison: "Oh my goodness! Doesn't he know the first thing about love? Doesn't he know he's always supposed to let the girl pick? That's how you honor a girl!"

Your kids are watching you, and listening. What a treat to hear them live these keys in the real world!

Forgive

Our third key is: I will learn every way possible to forgive my family members each day and seek forgiveness when I offend any one of them. I promise to help each family member remain in harmony as much as I'm able.

THE ABILITY TO FORGIVE STARTS WITH CHRIST—ALLOW HIM TO FORGIVE THROUGH YOU.

Forgiveness is not a feeling; it's a choice. "But I can't forgive," I've often heard. "This offense is too big." And I typically respond, "You're right. It is."

The ability to forgive starts with Christ—allow Him to forgive through you. Don't try to forgive in your own strength. Pray, "Lord, I know I need to forgive, but I can't. I'm willing to *want* to forgive. Please help me with this first step."

He will help you. You see, forgiveness is based on honor—honoring God, honoring His creation, and honoring ourselves.

Treasure Hunting

Our fourth key is about hidden treasure: I will take personal responsibility to find the pearls and God's blessings from each and every trial I face.

Here's a story from our daughter, Kari:

PAIN TURNED TO TREASURE

At age six, my daughter, Hannah, started praying for a baby sister. She was relentless in persuading us to open our hearts to adoption. Roger and I had lost a son prematurely and both of us were brokenhearted. We couldn't get beyond the pain.

Hannah would pray that God would provide the money we needed, open the door, and bring her a sister. She prayed fervently for over five years.

Somewhere along the way, our pain turned into a treasure. The prayers of our daughter melted our hearts and gave us renewed hope for the future—being a mom and dad again though adoption.

One of our proudest moments was when a beautiful baby girl named Zoie Senait was placed in Hannah's arms in Ethiopia. God answered her prayers in a big way and grew our family to five.

When you treasure hunt, you'll see the past differently. You'll see the present and future differently, too!

Abiding in the Words of Christ

Our fifth key is: I will learn and understand the Words of Christ and seek God's power to daily live His words.

When Jesus Christ is your Master, the Holy Spirit will live in you, and help you understand His words. Here's a story from Michael and Amy's son, Cole.

HIS WORDS ARE A LIGHT TO MY PATH

During my first three months of a gap-year program up in the Sequoia National Forest, my roommate had feelings for another girl in the program. We weren't allowed to date in this program, so for him this was really difficult. Meanwhile, this girl had broken the rules of the program and left to go home early.

This news hit my roommate hard. He immediately left the meeting after getting the news and called his parents. I could see he had been crying, so I knew the conversation he was having.

I could hear his mom on the other end of the phone, giving the best advice she could. There came a point when she asked what he was going to do next, and he said, "I'll probably talk to our resident director and Cole."

She said that sounded like a good idea but added, "I'm just not sure how mature Cole is."

When he hung up I told him to get some good shoes on, a good jacket, and a beanie. While he was busy doing this I put a Bible into my jacket. Late at night, with a flashlight, we walked fifteen minutes up the mountain. It was quiet there, and the stars were bright.

Reaching the top, I handed my roommate the flashlight and the Bible. As much as I love comforting, listening, and giving advice; I knew that this time it wasn't up to me to do that.

As I handed him the Bible I told him "No other human can hear you up here, and you don't need to be anywhere, so start talking, praying, crying, or whatever—and it better be out loud!"

Sometimes as mentors, or parents, we think we're supposed to be the ones God uses to speak to people. But the fact of the matter is that He wants to do the speaking Himself, sometimes through His Word.

Through this experience, not only did my friend learn to go to his heavenly Father for comfort, but I also learned how fun it was to listen for the Father's ideas.

Remember the Five M's

You've heard it said, "Marriage takes work." I never liked that expression. How about you? I prefer "Great marriages and joyful generations require intentionality."

As we review the five M's, think of them as ways of being intentional about your relationships. As we've said, the grace of God is our primary source of strength and hope. But we must make our own wise choices if we truly want a better life and a healthier family.

The sixth key is: I agree to live by the five M's: **(1)** honor my Master, **(2)** honor His mission for me, **(3)** understand my methods in this mission, **(4)** learn what works to move forward, and **(5)** value my mate (present or future mate).

MASTER

When we decide to establish Christ and His words as Master of our lives, what He says is what we do. It's decided.

Our Master, Jesus, made love a priority. He said the two greatest commands are to love God and to love others (Matthew 22:37–39). Not only does Jesus tell us to love, He gives us the very ability to love, and the miracle power to forgive.

Not only did He command us to honor our families, He first honored us with His love.

> "GREAT MARRIAGES AND JOYFUL GENERATIONS REQUIRE INTENTIONALITY."

Our first response, and responsibility, is to humble ourselves and believe His ways are right and the best for us. On behalf of the entire Smalley family, I hope you'll join us in humbling yourself and making Jesus Christ your Master.

MISSION

If you don't have your life's mission figured out, don't worry. We all share the mission of living these seven keys! The rest of your mission will become clearer as you build a solid foundation of honor and forgiveness.

Your heart's desires are not mere whims; consistent interest points toward your particular calling. Keep seeking and ask God to show you steps to your mission! As you do, involve your spouse and kids on your journey and talk about their mission, too.

Ask your kids what they're passionate about. Pay attention to activities your spouse migrates towards. Take note of what makes them excited about getting up in the morning. Ask them questions and explore these areas with them.

God has a special future in mind for you and your family!

METHODS

As with mission, you have the God-given honor of exploring and choosing possible methods to build a healthy family.

Here's a story from our daughter-in-law Amy:

A METHOD FOR OUR FAMILY

One of the methods Michael and I used, and still use, is to pay attention to our kids' unique strengths, so we can honor them.

For example, Reagan has always been a problem-solver. Because of that, Michael would purposely ask her questions about everyday happenings.

"Reagan, what are we going to do? We don't have any milk."

She'd pause and respond, "Daddy, we've got to go to the store. Come on, let's go!"

Instead of saying, "We have to go to the store to get milk," we tried to phrase things in a way that gave her opportunities to problem-solve.

Don't be afraid to try new methods, activities, and new conversations with your kids.

Yes, your first camping trip might be a disaster. Your first

LUV talk might lead to the biggest argument in history. Keep trying. Keep growing!

MOVE FORWARD

Maintain the good methods that seem to be working for your marriage and your kids. It's easier to rally in a crisis than to actually maintain a change. Why? When our home is in a peaceful routine, we have a tendency to breathe a sigh of relief and slip back into old habits.

Lasting growth happens, in you and your family, when you maintain methods that work. Keep your lists of each other's valuable qualities front-and-center.

Plan intentional time together outside the normal routine. When you do, you can be sure your family is moving forward, whether it feels like it or not!

YOUR MATE

If you're married, be an example to your spouse in the ways you put these keys into practice. Your kids will notice, too.

If you're single, choose a mate who is moving in the same direction as you are. Talk about Master, mission, and methods with a potential spouse. Pay attention to how that person "maintains" what they value. If you want harmony in your marriage, don't settle for a mate who isn't aligned with you and your mission.

Talk to your kids about marriage and about their future mate.

Marriage is a beautiful gift. With God's help, yours can shine brightly for all to see.

Up Close and Personal

One of our first camping experiences was in a simple pop-up

camper. Norma, our three little kids, and I, were all zipped in for the night, but weren't quite prepared for how cold Texas could get in the winter. Around eleven o'clock that night, I tried firing up a little heater. To my frustration, we were out of propane.

"No problem, we'll just sleep in our jackets," I suggested in my best lumberjack voice.

At 2:00 a.m. Norma and I were still awake and still freezing. By this time, she'd brought little Michael, who was about two years old, into her sleeping bag.

"I can't get him warm," she whispered, as Michael started crying. "We need to leave."

I had no interest in leaving because . . . it was cold! It was dark. I had a flashlight, but I would have to hook the trailer up to the car, connect all the electrical cords, and get everything packed.

Even though Michael was crying, the silence was deafening.

I crawled out from under the pile of blankets and jackets. Yes, I was grumbling to myself and stumbling around. Have you ever tried to pack up a campsite in the dark, with only a tiny flashlight?

As the sleepy campers settled into the overstuffed car, I was still silent.

Norma scooted over next to me, put her arm around me, kissed me and said, "You are my John Wayne."

I'll never forget that moment.

Warm memories are sometimes made in the most frigid circumstances. Here's our seventh key: I will try to meet face to face with as many family members as possible each year to remain bonded in harmony with them.

You have the tools, now take the time to make memories.

Joyful Generations

Yes, this book is about a thriving, loving marriage. And yes, this book is about parenting, bonded in harmony with direction and honor. But let's think bigger. Bigger than the argument you just had with your spouse . . . bigger than this morning's aggravating incident with your child.

Family was designed to go on forever. Not just the family tree—a family legacy!

Imagine building a legendary marriage—legendary to your kids and grandkids. Imagine your great-great-grandchildren recounting tales of you and your spouse. Picture family traditions, which you initiated, passed down for one hundred years. Two hundred years!

Does this perspective change your sense of family and mission?

Does this view make you see your Master differently?

You can lay the foundation for generations of honor.

Our family is cheering you on!

—— 11 ——

CHEERING TOGETHER

S ome people might say I've had nothing to cheer about since I began writing this book. But I've been wowed by the response of my family over the last seven months.

It all started in July of 2014, when I was in Hawaii speaking at a church. I love taking walks there, but for some reason I was completely exhausted.

Making my way up a little hill I thought, *something is wrong.* I called my grandson, described my symptoms, and had him call my cardiologist for some advice.

Walking back down the hill towards the hotel, the phone rang.

"I want you to take a nitroglycerin pill and then try to walk up the hill. I'll stay on the line," the doctor said.

I carried these pills around with me ever since my turkey-hunt incident, so I put the pill under my tongue, took a deep breath, and walked right up the hill with no strain.

"You're clogged!" he said.

As soon as I got back to the hotel, we made plans to get home and on to Atlanta with my grandson to see the cardiologist. I kept those pills handy.

Stress Test

After an examination at the Atlanta hospital, a procedure was scheduled for the very next day. When I woke up from surgery, I was surrounded by several members of my family. They informed me that my heart required several bypasses . . . and that I was

MEANINGFUL LIFE IS ALL ABOUT LOVING RELATIONSHIPS. EVERYTHING ELSE IS JUST DETAILS.

blessed to be alive. I still felt the same peace I'd experienced on that hill years before. And I wanted to see all my grandkids—as soon as possible.

I never imagined I'd see so much of them, and my kids, over the next several weeks. In fact, I had continuous companionship during many months of hospitalization.

After several ups-and-downs in my recovery, and some scary reports from medical experts, we realized I needed to move—across the country to live with my son Michael and his family.

Now I was feeling a different emotion. Yes, peace was always there, but I'd never experienced such honor before. I felt extremely valued by my wife, kids, and everyone in our family.

And yes, I felt a bit uncomfortable at the prospect of being cared for by my family—especially in my son's home.

I've been writing, teaching, and speaking about family for over forty years. I've been leading my family for longer than that. But now I was on the receiving end of all that I had tried to teach.

My Trial and My Treasure

Meaningful life is all about loving relationships. Everything else is just details. I know I'm highly loved by God, and I accept the value He places on me. He has been faithful to me and my family. I have been relying on Him and His living Words to guide me through all circumstances, including the circumstance of major medical challenges, while moving in with my son's family.

My life centers around loving God, loving my family, and loving as many people as I can along the way. This book is another expression of that love!

I choose to keep my anger level as low as possible by forgiving everyone every day. Because I practice this action, I'm becoming more skilled at using negative, hurtful experiences for good.

Finding the good in everything that is "bad" is my favorite way to keep my anger at the lowest levels.

If I'm in a big trial, I first feel the pain and the magnitude of the trial, because that's part of finding how I'm being benefited. I'm not feeling fear today but mostly hope about my future because of how faithful and amazing God has been to answer my prayers. My kids and grandkids have watched this old man pray their entire lives, and they've seen the impossible happen.

Now my son and his family are seeing the unexpected happen.

Here's my son Michael's perspective:

HOME TOGETHER AGAIN

At our house, when my family talks about our *surprise guest*, I remind them of how things could have been.

Dad came from a dysfunctional home. He could easily have taken us down that road. Things would have been completely different for him and for us. Our family might have been full of anger. But Dad decided to take on the responsibility to lead us. He decided to live the greatest commandment: love God with all your heart, soul, mind, and strength.

And then he built the relational side by investing in each of us. So, what we've seen these past seven months is us doing family together. This is what Mom and Dad always wanted, but maybe not *how* we expected it to happen.

We have our family pledge, which comes in pretty handy some days!

Dad's health challenges could have strained our family to the breaking point. But instead, there's been a collaboration, rallying around what's best for him. Are we superhuman? Ha! Far from it!

It's also important to note that there's plenty for Mom and Dad to be upset about—tons! He gets discouraged sometimes, but those feelings don't last very long. I see him hold tight to these seven keys, like we have all our lives. And it's an honor for my kids to see this in action.

Yes, taking care of Dad has been really stressful at times, but love and honor have been *baked* into our family. It's who we are.

The Fruit of Honor

I'm living in a new season, and so is our family. For my kids and their mates, it's a new season in marriage—seeing each other care for a parent—me! And our grandkids get to see what it really means to honor parents and lift up grandparents.

> **IT'S SO IMPORTANT FOR KIDS TO KNOW THAT A FAMILY TAKES CARE OF EACH OTHER.**

Speaking of being lifted up, during this recovery, I sometimes need some help getting off the couch. A few weeks ago, my grandson David pulled me up so hard that I almost knocked him over!

He's getting stronger. We all are.

It's so important for kids to know that a family takes care of each other. This is what life's all about. We've had a big opportunity to hunt for treasure together these past few months.

As a parent, you might not have put much thought into your later years and how you'll be cared for. If you're a grandparent, like me, you probably have. As they grow older, many people have a fear of dependency. They don't want to impose or be a burden. Or worse—they wonder if their family will honor them.

I hoped mine would, but now I know they will—because they are! Every one of them. By the grace of God, Norma and I are reaping the fruit of honor.

Choose to Cheer

You are brave. You're a bold dreamer. How do I know? Well, if you've read this far, you're dreaming of a better family. Not

HAVING A GRATEFUL HEART IS THE WILL OF GOD.

only better relationships now, but for generations to come.

You already know that the concept of family is under attack. You recognize the deadly infection of anger. You see some of the logs in your own eye, and you're humbling yourself to build family relationships worth repeating.

You dare to believe that your family can grow together in harmony, and you are taking new steps together.

My family and I are cheering you on!

Does your family resemble some picture-perfect vacation brochure—all smiles and laughter? Mine usually doesn't. But we choose to rejoice along the way.

Let me share one more ingredient for a healthy family: choose to cheer.

Cheering by Faith

Cheering is honoring. Cheering energizes all seven keys. And cheering is a choice.

We all need to celebrate more—even during trials. Especially during trials! I understand it may feel impossible, but cheering is an act of faith and trust in God. It's an act of honoring God's Word and believing that He is faithful. Jesus said these words:

"These things I have spoken unto you, that in me ye might have peace. In the world ye shall have tribulation: but be of good cheer; I have overcome the world." (John 16:33 KJV)

I don't cheer the pain, but I can cheer the benefits I'm going to get. I know the pearls are forming, and I'm on the lookout for them!

Having a grateful heart is the will of God. Why does Jesus tell us to rejoice in our trials? At first, it didn't make sense to me, so I looked up the original Greek word for rejoice. One of the definitions is "to give a cheer."

Nobody feels like cheering in difficult situations. I didn't feel like cheering after my heart attack years ago, and I didn't feel like cheering through all the operations and procedures I've been through the past seven months.

But I've practiced. I do the will of God, no matter how I feel. And I ask for God's help. It's actually possible to change your whole outlook on a situation if you'll start to cheer. We don't cheer the trials—we cheer the treasures that God can work in the process!

As you start to use these keys with your family, two kinds of results will occur . . . good stuff and bad stuff. Cheer in both situations.

All Things Can Work for Good

As you take steps to honor, to forgive, and to help family members release anger, I want you to have the right expectations. You'll make mistakes along the way. Family members might sometimes react in disappointing ways.

Remember that one of the main causes of anger is unmet expectations. If you have unrealistic expectations, you'll set yourself up for unnecessary heartache. But if you'll adopt God's expectations you can have hope, peace, joy, and love.

Even when focusing on our marriage, we must see the bigger picture: generations of healthy families! This is possible with God's help, and this begins with you.

God will eventually restore pure goodness to all creation. He promises to turn everything into something good for you, because you love Him and you're called according to His purpose (Romans 8:28).

This is the hope we can adopt: If a situation is causing frustration or pain, we can actually thank God for His goodness, and cheer. Blessings, growth, and breakthroughs are all working their way into our family.

Jesus told us to expect trials, and in the same breath He instructed us to be of good cheer:

> Blessed are those who are persecuted because of righteousness, for theirs is the kingdom of heaven. Blessed are you when people insult you, persecute you and falsely say all kinds of evil against you because of me. Rejoice and be glad, because great is your reward in heaven. (Matthew 5:10–12)

Rejoice in difficult times? What a concept—and what a way to live! I wish someone would have told me about cheering fifty years ago!

> A miserable heart means a miserable life; a cheerful heart fills the day with song. (Proverbs 15:15, *The Message*)

Solomon wrote the proverb, but Norma taught this truth to me. She's always singing songs of thankfulness to God.

Patience and Persistence

Be patient with yourself, with your spouse, and with your kids. Keep the words of Christ in your mind. The race we're running is not a sprint.

I know God is working good for me. I know there's an ultimate goodness coming my way. So I cheer! Yes, I realize this might seem like a bizarre concept, or at least a new concept.

> **FEAR IS PICTURING YOUR FUTURE WITHOUT GOD. FAITH IS KNOWING YOUR FUTURE IS WITH GOD.**

Of course my initial, natural reaction to hurt or disappointment isn't cheerful. But I rejoice out of obedience—my Master told me to, and He wants the best for me. I cheer as long as it takes for my perspective to shift into hope.

I celebrate by faith. When God gives a promise to work all things together for good, that's something big to celebrate! Therefore, I can cheer during difficult times, knowing the situation is in the process of being turned into something good for me.

Cheer Leaders

When a football team scores a touchdown, every fan cheers. And that's good! But the real power of cheering comes into play when your team is struggling.

When your family team is having a hard day or a tough month, you must choose to cheer.

Fear is picturing your future without God. Faith is knowing your future is with God. You can't cheer and be stressed at the same time. You can't be thankful and angry at the same time. So why not choose to cheer?

When you really think about it, cheering is a form of treasure hunting—you're looking for goodness in the midst of hardship. Treasure hunting is honoring how God can turn all things for good.

Today's thoughts will shape tomorrow's actions—and reactions. So teach your family to cheer together!

Here's another story from our son Michael . . .

CHEERING NORMA

For us three kids, Mom was a phenomenal cheer-leader, in every sense of the word.

In high school, I played football all four years. She was at almost every game, and most of the practices. Whose mom comes to practice? But for some reason, her being there never bothered me. And the team loved hearing her shouts of encouragement.

During those years she only missed one game. My teammates noticed, asking, "Hey, where's your mom? We don't hear her cheering."

I think that says a lot.

People who cheer are sorely missed when they're not around.

Mom is a private person, but you'd never have known it at football games, or with anything her family was involved in. She made a big impact on me, the team, and all my classmates, by cheering.

I hope I'm remembered as a dad, son, husband, and brother who cheers. And I hope I let the people cheering around me know that they're appreciated.

Cheering to Remember

You might be thinking, Where do I start establishing these seven keys in my family? I can't even remember them all!

Your most vivid memories are emotional memories. That's why most people only remember about 5 percent of what they learned in school, because there wasn't an emotional connection to most of the information.

Do you know why women tend to know every detail of a heated argument from ten years ago—and remember what their husband was wearing when it happened? It's because they experience situations on a deeper emotional level than men.

Emotions drive memory, for both men and women. As you review these pillars, whether personally or with your spouse, picture the transformational impact each will have on your family. Imagine the joy and sense of security that honor will unlock in your marriage.

Feel the sadness and anger from past hurts, and forgive—emotionally. Forgive yourself, as God your Master has forgiven you.

Experience the power and beauty in the words of Christ. Sometimes I even get teary-eyed as I see God's amazing love for us expressed in His Word. The more emotional I become in memorizing a verse and a truth, the longer I remember it.

Cheer yourself on as you begin to hunt for pearls. Cheer your family on as they begin to treasure each other.

Rejoice when the campfire scorches your dinner beyond recognition. Smile in the midst of rained-out picnics.

You're making memories together and traditions of love and honor.

Love Letters

This book is a love letter from my family to *you* and to *your family*. We hope you'll refer to these seven keys often. Go back through the book from time to time and keep it handy as a guide.

We've been on this journey for many years, and our family still isn't perfect—but we love each other and we see joyful generations ahead. We're cheering you on!

This book is also a love letter to my family.

These pillars and stories are for the family I know and love—and the family I've not yet known in future generations.

I love you all.

It brings me amazing joy to picture you reading this book and relating these stories to your children's children.

I'm cheering you on!

APPENDIX

THE SMALLEY/GIBSON FAMILY PLEDGE

1. I will learn to highly honor and love each family member.
2. I will learn to keep my anger to the lowest level each day toward every family member or in any situation.
3. I will learn every way possible to forgive my family members each day and seek forgiveness when I offend any one of them. I promise to help each family member remain in harmony as much as I'm able.
4. I will take personal responsibility to find the pearls and God's blessings from each and every trial I face.
5. I will learn and understand the words of Christ and seek God's power to daily live His words.
6. I agree to live by the 5 M's: I will honor my Master, honor His mission for me and my methods in this mission, learn what works to move forward, and value my mate (present or future mate).
7. I will try to meet face to face with as many family members as possible each year to remain bonded in harmony with them.

FOUR ROCKS

There are so many powerful truths and life-changing promises found in the Bible. Let's begin the way I began, with four pocket-size "rocks."

1. "Blessed are the poor in spirit, for theirs is the kingdom of heaven."(Matthew 5:3)

2. "'Love the Lord your God with all your heart and with all your soul and with all your mind and with all your strength.' The second is this: 'Love your neighbor as yourself.' There is no commandment greater than these." (Mark 12:30–31)

3. "As the Father has loved me, so have I loved you. Now remain in my love. If you keep my commands, you will remain in my love, just as I have kept my Father's commands and remain in his love. I have told you this so that my joy may be in you and that your joy may be complete. My command is this: Love each other as I have loved you." (John 15:9–12)

4. "Blessed are those who are persecuted because of righteousness, for theirs is the kingdom of heaven. Blessed are you when people insult you, persecute you and falsely say all kinds of evil against you because of me. Rejoice and be glad, because great is your reward in heaven, for in the same way they persecuted the prophets who were before you." (Matthew 5:10–12)

ENDNOTES

1. http://en.wikipedia.org/wiki/The_Notorious_ Cherry_Bombs
2. Caroline Leaf, *Switch on Your Brain* (Grand Rapids, MI: Baker, 2013), 34.
3. http://en.wikipedia.org/wiki/Pearl
4. Steven K. Scott is the author of *The Greatest Words Ever Spoken: Everything Jesus Said About You, Your Life, and Everything Else.*
5. Leaf, *Switch On Your Brain*, 111.
6. http://thefamilydinnerproject.org/about-us/ benefits-of-family-dinners/

ACKNOWLEDGEMENTS

This book represents what Norma and I have learned throughout the fifty years of ups and downs in our marriage and family, which have only been sustained and nurtured by God's unending grace. I would like to show my deepest appreciation to John Mason and Mike Loomis, gifted writers, who captured the heart of my family's legacy and painted a beautiful picture of God's love in and through my family.

Special acknowledgement also goes to the National Leadership and Resource Center of the Assemblies of God General Council executive leadership team, Sol and Wini Arledge, Steve and Susan Blount, and their team. Not only do they understand the value of strengthening families as a primary source of discipleship, they also vigorously work to further God's kingdom through resourcing homes and churches to empower families for today and tomorrow. Heaven rejoices because of their hard work!

Finally, this work would not have been completed without the participation of my kids and grandkids. Norma and I cherish being your parents and grandparents. We're confident that you'll carry on our family legacy as you continue to live lives that are honoring to God.

ABOUT THE AUTHOR

Gary Smalley is one of the country's best known authors and speakers on family relationships. He is the author and coauthor of sixteen bestselling, award-winning books along with several popular films and videos. He has spent over thirty years learning, teaching, and counseling. Gary has personally interviewed hundreds of singles and couples and has surveyed thousands of people at his seminars, asking two questions: What is it that strengthens your relationships? and, What weakens them?

Gary's books combined have sold over five million copies. Many of them have been translated into various languages. *The Blessing* and *The Two Sides of Love* have won the Gold Medallion Award for excellence in literature. *The Language of Love* won the Angel Award as the best contribution to family life. All other titles have been top-five finalists for the Gold Medallion Award.

Gary Smalley has appeared on national television programs such as *Oprah, Larry King Live, Extra, The Today Show,* and *Sally Jessy Raphael,* as well as numerous national radio programs. Gary has been featured on hundreds of regional and local television and radio programs across the United States.

Gary and his wife, Norma, have been married for over fifty years and live in Colorado Springs. They have three children, Kari, Greg, and Michael, and ten grandchildren.

FOR MORE INFORMATION

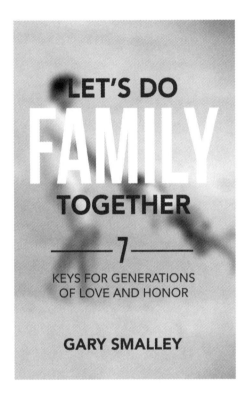

For more information about this book and other valuable resources visit www.salubrisresources.com

248.8 SMA

Let's do family together : Smalley,
Gary,

39061003403398

Sep 2015

ADAMS COUNTY PUBLIC LIBRARY
NORTH ADAMS   ACN